Terry Culbe[rt]

Lucan
HOME OF THE DONNELLYS

WESTERN HOTEL Jos FORREST Prop.

Published by

GENERAL STORE
PUBLISHING HOUSE

499 O'Brien Rd., Box 415, Renfrew, Ontario, Canada K7V 4A6
Telephone (613) 432-7697 or 1-800-465-6072
www.gsph.com

ISBN 1-897113-31-5

Printing by Custom Printers of Renfrew Ltd.

Printed and bound in Canada

Illustrations and photographs by the author.
Cover design, formatting and printing by Custom Printers of Renfrew Ltd.
Front cover photo courtesy University of Western Ontario Archives.
Back cover illustration courtesy of the Lucan Area Heritage Donnelly Museum.

Library and Archives Canada Cataloguing in Publication Data

Culbert, Terry, 1942 -
    Terry Culbert's Lucan : Home of the Donnellys : Linger Longer in Lovely Lucan / Terry Culbert.

Includes bibliographical references.
ISBN 1-897113-31-5

    1. Lucan (Ont.)--History.   I. Title.

FC3099.L82C84 2005   971.3'25   C2005-905611-8

First Printing November 2005
Second Printing February 2006

Dedication

To my darling Barbara.
You made writing this book a wonderful experience.
Your constant support and encouragement,
your research and edits, made creating
my second book a joy.

Contents

Foreword

As a young boy growing up on our Roman Line family farm, I looked forward to shopping trips into Lucan. I treasure the memories of visiting Terry's parents' Dry Goods and Variety Store in the 1950s. Among my most vivid memories of the store was the friendly atmosphere and great inventory of toys. Therefore, it strikes me as fitting that Terry, one of Lucan's successful sons, has decided to author a collection of short stories about his hometown. *Lucan, Home of the Donnellys* is a refreshing look at the Donnelly saga, village commerce, village life, sports, and music. I know this will be an enjoyable read for many. Thanks, Terry!

Tom McLaughlin
Mayor, Lucan Biddulph

Acknowledgements

There are people who willingly give support in one form or another when one embarks on a project like this. My family members were more than willing—they were remarkable. A heartfelt thank you to Aunt Muriel Culbert in Lucan for giving me the inspiration to write this book and for letting me stay at her lovely home, affectionately known by the family as the Rosevilla Bed and Breakfast.

A very special thank you to my life partner, Barbara Hoegenauer, my first editor and advisor, who never wavered in her support and encouragement. Where I would gather the nuts and bolts for my stories, Barbara had the patience and ability to make the stories flow cohesively.

Thank you to my sister Mary Jane Culbert in Vancouver for a great deal of research, and my sister Dana Garrett in London for research and for lodging when Aunt Muriel was away; and to my darling daughters, Sarah Renda and Dana Johnson, for giving me bed and breakfast when researching and interviewing in their areas.

To Doug Ovens, Sheila Hodgins, Ruth Grice, and Don Froats of the Lucan Area Heritage Society, thank you for all your contributions. A big thank you to Harry Hardy of Lucan, and Casey Markus of Regina-based Partners in Motion, for all their help.

Finally, I would like to thank Tim Gordon and his staff, Rosemary Nugent, Ann Conway, and Ann Forgie at General Store Publishing House in Renfrew, Ontario, as well as their Kingston editor, Jane Karchmar, for their support. Thanks also to Tara Yourth and Cathy Appleyard of Custom Printers. It would have been difficult to complete this project without the co-operation of a lot of people. Thank you all!

Introduction

My first compilation of stories, entitled *County Roads,* was published in 1995. At the time, I was Global Television's first cameraman-reporter. I was self-assigning and had the freedom to travel the province of Ontario, producing positive lifestyle stories. Over the past decade, I have put pen to paper and two fingers to my keyboard various times. Nothing ever came of it until February of 2003 when my Aunt Muriel Culbert invited me to be the guest speaker at the Lucan Heritage Dinner.

Aunt Muriel's son, my cousin Jeff, actor and artistic director of the Ausable Theatre Company, introduced me to the audience. Jeff gave me the finest welcome I have ever received. As he strummed his guitar and sang "Galway Bay," I was touched and thrilled to be in my old hometown, which has always held a special place in my heart. Lucan has a very rich, albeit controversial, history and has generated a lot of curiosity over the years. That evening I shared my experience growing up in this Irish-Canadian village with the audience, who received me with a lot of enthusiasm.

The following morning, Aunt Muriel suggested I put my many varied anecdotes into book form. During my trip home, I was consumed with thoughts of writing about Lucan. A jumble of ideas and stories raced through my mind. All I needed now was the support of my life partner, Barbara, whose only reaction was: "What's stopping you?"

Maps

Lucan, County Dublin, Ireland
County Tipperary, Ireland
Township of Lucan-Biddulph, Canada

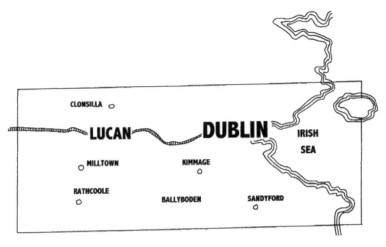

Lucan, County Dublin, Ireland

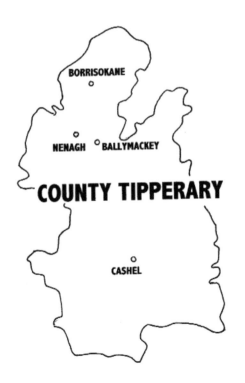

County Tipperary, Ireland

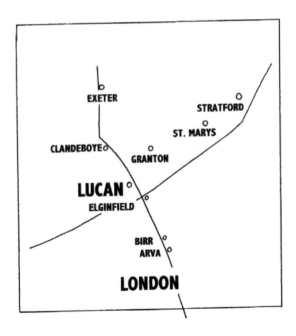

Township of Lucan-Biddulph, Canada

PART ONE: *Early History*

Early History

Lucan's Main Street, complete with residential homes, commercial buildings, and the hustle and bustle of local shoppers, was once a heavily travelled trail by First Nation people heading north or south. This densely wooded region was known as Attawondron or Neutrals Territory. The area, rich in history, holds a great interest for the Museum of Indian Archaeology in London, Ontario, which was established by Amos and Wilfrid Jury in 1933.

Archaeologists continue to study the occupation of the City of London and Southern Ontario by native people. The excavation sites provide us with a glimpse into how people have lived over the past 11,000 years. In 1990, William D. Finlayson, Robert J. Pearce, Peter A. Timmins, and Bern Wheeler collaborated in researching and writing a special presentation entitled: *London, Ontario—The First 11,000 Years.*

Archaeological evidence, according to The London [Ontario] Museum of Archaeology, suggests that the first people crossed the Bering Strait from Asia before the tenth millennium BC. By 9,000 BC, after the glaciers retreated and the tundra-like environment appeared, the first human inhabitants arrived in southwestern Ontario.

The period from 1,000 BC to 300 BC has been termed the Early Woodland Period, a time of widespread burial rites, where gravesites contained a multitude of artefacts. The Early Woodland Period saw a surge in stone toolmaking technology, and arrowheads found on the Early Woodland sites are so finely made that some archaeologists believe they were manufactured by a few highly skilled craftsmen. They were widely exchanged within a broad trade network that extended over much of northeastern North America.

The Middle Woodland Period, from 300 BC to 800 AD, saw further increases in population and the development of more complex social and political systems. Middle Woodland bands occupied most of the major river drainages in southwestern Ontario, including a major occupation of the Thames. Living in large groups at prime fishing locations along the Thames River during the spring and summer, these bands then dispersed into smaller groups and moved to inland camps for the fall and winter. In London, inland fall and winter camps were located on the Ingersoll Moraine near ponds and bogs in the Byron and Pond Mills areas. Around 500 AD, corn first made its appearance in Southern Ontario.

The Late Woodland Period started around 800 AD with a growing emphasis on agriculture and the cultivation of corn, beans, and squash. Late Woodland bands were the direct ancestors to the historically known Iroquoian confederacies: the Huron and the Neutral.

THE CANADA COMPANY,

Have nearly One Million Acres of Land,

OF THE FINEST DESCRIPTION,

For Sale, in the Huron Tract,

And persons desirous of purchasing can obtain all the necessary information, as to prices, situation of vacant Lots, and mode of application, from the *Land Agents,* appointed for that purpose, at the Company's Offices in,

Goderich, Stratford, & Hay.

The object which the Canada Company have principally in view in appointing those Agents, is that they may afford the information, for they have not been empowered to receive Money; persons, therefore, having to make payments, either on account of credit Instalments falling due, or first Instalments on new purchases, may lodge the money with the Bank of Upper Canada Agency in the *Town of London,* on account of the Canada Company, who will give them a Receipt for the same, which may be remitted to the Commissioners in Toronto as *Cash,* and by return of Post its receipt will be acknowledged; or should there be no Bank Agency in the neighbourhood, they may retain the money till the arrival of one of the Commissioners, who will attend at each Agency every second month, for the purpose of receiving money and issuing Location Tickets to purchasers; or they may forward the amount, at their own risk, by the Post from *Stratford* or *Goderich,* and which leaves the latter place twice each week for Toronto.

No person will be allowed to take up Land who is not prepared to *pay the first Instalment in Cash,* either by remittance in the manner here pointed out, or to the Commissioner on his periodical visits, and should this regulation not be complied with, the Lands will be immediately held as open for re-sale; nor will any person be allowed to hold Land who has not made a regular application for it through the Land Agent, and received his written permission to take possession of it on the terms here stated.

Canada Company's Office,
Toronto, 1st May, 1836.

Printed at the U. C. Gazette Office.

Wilberforce Settlement

Wilberforce was one of Canada's first black settlements. After Lieutenant Governor Simcoe's 1793 legislation banning slavery in Upper Canada, the word spread in the Southern United States that Canada was a safe haven for blacks. Free blacks from Cincinnati, Ohio, and Boston, Massachusetts, established the Wilberforce Settlement in 1829. Named after British abolitionist William Wilberforce, the colony extended from the Ausable River through what is now the village of Lucan and as far south as the London–Biddulph town line. Those early beginnings of black settlements in Upper Canada were mostly successful, as the new pioneers had much to offer. For example, tobacco farming was introduced by new blacks from Kentucky and Virginia. The Canada Company agreed to sell 4,000 acres of land for $6,000, approximately $1.50 per acre, to the new settlers.

The black pioneers went to work for the land surveyors, cutting timber and clearing roadways. They worked tremendously hard, in the process helping to open up the Township of Biddulph. The settlers cleared dense forests, which was gruelling work, in a desperate attempt to set up their own farmsteads. The Wilberforce community grew to include thirty-two families. Unfortunately, in 1830, a lack of funds and assistance made it difficult for colonists to make the obligatory payments to the Canada Company.

Help came in the form of the Quakers, a religious order who tried to assist the struggling pioneers by purchasing land and donating it back to the black settlers. The Quakers were known to be sympathetic to fugitive slaves and played a great part in the Underground Railroad, a network of secret routes through which slaves could escape to the Northern States and into Canada. Regrettably, this act of brotherly love was doomed to failure. The Quakers were unable to raise sufficient funds and were able to purchase only 800 acres. This did not satisfy the Canada Company, and by 1835, twelve of the thirty-two black families were forced to return to the United States.

The Wilberforce Settlement was not deemed a success. Due to poor management, a shortfall of settlers, and prejudice by some neighbours, Wilberforce lasted only six years.

All that remains today is the Butler family and a cemetery bearing their name. Edward Clifford Butler was born on the 14th of January, 1926, and still resides in Lucan. His brother Harold Joseph Sydney Butler, born July 28th, 1923, lives in the nearby City of London. Harold and Ed's great-great-grandfather, Peter Butler, was among the first settlers to arrive in Wilberforce. Peter was born in 1797 in Baltimore, Maryland. He and his wife, Salome, purchased Lot 5 on the London–Goderich Road and raised seven children. Peter's hard-working family had amassed close to a thousand acres of land, which included most of the present village of Lucan.

As far back as anyone can remember, the Butlers had always been interested in herbal healing. Peter himself had a vast knowledge of herbal medicine, which was passed on through generations by his family. He became known as "Doc" Butler, serving his community as a self-appointed doctor. His son Peter Butler II inherited his father's knowledge of herbal medicine, and both men were called upon to care for the area's sick regardless of skin colour. Harold and Ed's grandfather, Peter Butler III, was born in 1859 and was a police constable for sixty-one years before his death in 1943. Legend has it that Peter was the only person who had the fortitude to act as a constable in the Lucan district after the Donnelly massacre. "He was a big man, standing six feet tall, weighing 187 pounds. He feared no one," said his grandson Ed. "He had amazing energy and was good with his fists. He relied on his size to keep the peace and supposedly carried a gun only when transporting prisoners or chasing cattle rustlers. He occasionally carried a big stick when his size and force of personality were not enough to maintain peace."

Nevertheless, he was known for his generosity. Every Saturday night, Butler would purchase a large bucket of beer for the inmates held in the Lucan jail. In 1921, a tribute to Peter Butler III was published in the *London Free Press*. "No favouritism was shown any lawbreakers, but all received just treatment at the hands of the Lucan constable." Peter Butler III

Photo courtesy University of Western Ontario Archives

Constable Peter Butler III

was also the first black officer with the Ontario Provincial Police.

I had the privilege to talk to the Butler brothers at the home of Ed and his wife, Annelies, in February 2004. I have personally known the Butler family since I was a six-year-old attending Lucan Public School with Harold's daughter Beverly.

**Wilberforce descendants
Harold and Ed Butler.**

During the Second World War, Harold served with the Royal Canadian Army Service Corps, stationed in London, Ontario, and Ed went overseas, eventually joining the Highland Light Infantry. "I married a gal from Holland," said Ed. "Her name was Nicoline Krul and we had four children together." Sadly, Nicoline died in 1963, and Ed was left to raise four children. He happily accepted the help offered by his wife's niece Annelies, who arrived from Holland to support the family. Annelies stayed, and a few years later married Ed. "Yes, I married my uncle," she said with a chuckle. "We have four children as well, and Ed is a grandfather twenty-one times."

Not to be outdone, Harold married at the tender age of nineteen and he and wife Doris had two daughters and an adopted son. "After Doris passed away, I married Jean, a retired nurse," explained Harold. "Between the two of us we have twenty-eight grandchildren and thirteen great-grandchildren."

The brothers have always been self-employed. They were in the scrap metal business and also installed hundreds of weeping tile beds and septic tanks throughout Biddulph Township. "Harold and I have worked our whole lives together; we always got along," said Ed. It is obvious that both men are basking in the comfort of their large families. "Family and church are extremely important to me," said Ed. "When I came home from overseas, I turned my life over to the Lord and I have been consistent in my faith all these years. I'm more interested in where I'm going than where I've been."

On Sunday, August 28th, 1966, a historical plaque was unveiled in Lucan to commemorate the pioneer black Wilberforce Settlement. It was erected by the Province of Ontario's Department of Tourism and Information.

Wilberforce Settlement Becomes Marystown

During the early 1800s, immigrants, for the most part Irish, began arriving in Biddulph Township. Due to hardships, the black pioneers of the Wilberforce Settlement began to leave, making room for the Irish settlers. John McDonald and his nephew Donald McDonald were hired by the Canada Company to survey the area. At that time, the Canada Company preferred to pay their surveyors in grants of land rather than cash. The McDonalds had no problem with that arrangement, completing their surveys of the area around 1840.

By the time the McDonalds' work was done, they and Peter "Doc" Butler, who was hired to help clear the land, owned the majority of the lots in the settlement. The three men did well monetarily by selling property to the Grand Trunk Railway as it was being built across Biddulph. It was reported that on the death of "Doc" Butler in 1872, he was worth $22,000, a sizeable estate at that time.

John McDonald and his nephew Donald proceeded to change the name from Wilberforce Settlement to Marystown in honour of John's wife, Mary. John moved to Goderich, where he became the first sheriff of Huron County, and his nephew Donald moved to York (Toronto), where he was appointed a senator.

Photo courtesy University of Western Ontario Archives.

Henry Hunn and his horse.

Marystown Becomes Lucan

When it was discovered that Upper Canada had two villages named Marystown, the newer of the two in Biddulph Township was instructed by the post office to change its name. Lucan was incorporated as a village on January 1st, 1872.

While researching this book, I came across two schools of thought as to where the name "Lucan" originated. The records for the St. Patrick's Parish, just south of Marystown, claimed a number of prominent men in the community requested Father Peter Crinnon to change the village name. He named it Lucan in honour of the great Irish general, Patrick Sarsfield, who was thought to have been born in Lucan, County Dublin, around 1649. There is no record to prove his birth in that Irish village. As a matter of fact, the people of Tully, County Kildare, claim he was born and reared there. According to Irish historian Mary Mulhall, Patrick Sarsfield was likely born in Lucan, County Dublin, and left as a baby.

The other theory claims that an Irishman known as "Dublin" Tom Hodgins suggested naming the village after Lucan, County Dublin, as well.

Mary Mulhall, author of *Lucan and Lucanians: A Revised History of Lucan, County Dublin*, writes: "In 1829, a coachman from Lucan Demesne, a Thomas Hodgins, emigrated to Upper Canada, becoming the founder of a village named 'Lucan' in honour of his birthplace, hence the name Lucan in Biddulph Township." "Dublin" Tom Hodgins (1809–91) married Anne Shoebottom of London Township in 1838, and together they raised thirteen children. Tom entered local politics, eventually becoming the reeve of Biddulph Township in 1856 and 1857.

Growing up in an Irish-Canadian village played a great role in my love for history and travel. The urge to learn more about my background and ancestry impelled me to fly across the Atlantic to the United Kingdom and Ireland fifteen times. I visited the village of Lucan, County Dublin, on two occasions. The first time was in November of 1989. I was with my friend Wayne Brennan en route to visit his family in Ballymurry, County Roscommon. The second visit to Lucan took place in May of 1993, with the late Bob McAdorey. Bob and I were spending two weeks in Ireland producing a St. Patrick's Day special for Global Television.

Lucan is situated alongside the River Liffey, eight miles west of Dublin City. As Bob McAdorey and I entered the village, it appeared more beautiful than I had remembered. A blue and white phone booth caught my attention. Adorned with large Gaelic letters, it stood between the River Griffeen and a tree-lined street in the heart of the business district. Quaint stores, pubs, and a betting shop made up the downtown. As I walked through an alley between O'Neill's Lucan Inn and

The Irish Permanent Building Society, I could see the remains of the Church of the Blessed Virgin Mary looming above a graveyard as though standing on guard. In that same graveyard, I discovered the oldest legible headstone, bearing the name of Omar Kelly, who had died in 1692, a year after the Battle of the Boyne.

The Gaelic for Lucan is Leamhcán, thought to be derived from *Leamhean*, meaning "elm."

There are plenty of elm trees in the Irish Lucan. The Biddulph Lucan had its share of elm trees as well, although in 1915, a very old elm, a Lucan landmark, got in the way of a hydro crew and the decision was made to fell the obstacle. W.W. Revington, known as the Bard of Biddulph, poetically expressed his regret in seeing the tree cut down:

THE FAMOUS OLD ELM

Once near the place where stands today,
Ab Simpson's fine abode,
Stood Dinney Dorsey's blacksmith shop,
South of the London Road.
Near by his shop there once did stand
A famous elm tree;
It was indeed as fine an elm
As you would wish to see.
No wonder he admired that tree
And Dinney often said
That weary travellers turned in
To rest beneath its shade.
But now we hear some hydro men
By some means did contrive
To cut that tree. They never would
If Dinney were alive.
Where was Tom Benn, Joe Collision,
Or even Pat McGee?
To let those daring hydro men
Come there and cut that tree!

My second visit to Lucan, County Dublin, was in May 1993 with the late Bob McAdorey. We spent two weeks in Ireland producing a number of stories and a St. Patrick's Day special for Global Television.

PART TWO: *The Donnellys*

"When Hell Broke Loose
With fists and clubs they fought the Donnellys,
Under moon and sun.
In village streets and on sideroads–
Ah, but the Donnellys always won."

– Old Song.

Illustration by the author at age eighteen (1960).

Donnelly Family

Growing up in Lucan during the 1940s and '50s, I clearly remember its being strictly taboo to mention the Donnelly name. We were told that relatives of the Vigilantes involved in the massacre of February 4th, 1880, were still residing in the area. That information has always left me with a slight feeling of unease. It seems inconceivable that five people could be murdered by neighbours and so-called friends, and no one brought to justice.

In my late twenties, while working at CFPL Television in London, I ventured onto the Roman Line with news anchor Jack Burghardt to explore the area where the Donnellys had lived and died. We wandered between the tombstones in St. Patrick's graveyard, finding the Donnelly family marker. We learned that the original stone with the inscription "murdered" had been replaced with a stone marked "died."

In 1977, I discovered Ray Fazakas's book, *The Donnelly Album*. To my surprise, the Culbert name was listed four times in the index. My favourite anecdote from the book involves a distant relative named Thomas Culbert. He was a hotel and livery stable owner in nearby Granton, six miles from Lucan. Apparently, Tom Donnelly deliberately fixed a fight in order to collect some side bets. When Thomas Culbert and his one-armed friend Rhody Kennedy discovered the trick, they demanded their money back on

grounds of fraud. The two furious losers confronted Tom and Bob Donnelly as the pair of brothers swilled beer at Fitzhenry's Hotel in Lucan. The Donnelly lads told the two accusers to go to hell, and then proceeded to beat up Kennedy and Culbert. There is an old adage: *If you can't fight your way out of a wet paper bag, don't get into a fight!* To this day, Culberts are not fighters, they're lovers!

This chapter is an abbreviated version of the Donnelly story. It was never my intention to write extensively on the subject, but merely to add a chapter about the Donnelly family as part of Lucan's rich history. If you want to delve into this fascinating part of Canadiana, I highly recommend two books by Ray Fazakas: *The Donnelly Album* (1977) and *In Search of the Donnellys* (2001).

In Ireland's northern Tipperary town of Borrisokane, James Donnelly was born into the Catholic faith on the 7th day of March 1816. As James entered manhood, he began work as a coach driver. On one of his routes, he met a servant girl named Johannah Magee. James quickly developed a crush on Johannah, who not only was seven years younger, but was also raised a staunch Protestant. This was of no concern to James, but Johannah's father was incensed by the bourgeoning relationship. Mr. Magee did not give his blessing to the couple and was outraged when the pair eloped. He finally caught up with his newly married daughter, took her home against her will, and placed her under guard. Despite all of Mr. Magee's efforts, the young couple was eventually able to reunite. On the 8th of December 1841, Johannah, who was affectionately known as Judy, gave birth to a son they named James Donnelly Jr.

With the onset of the Potato Famine and a failing economy, James Senior decided to see what the New World had to offer. In 1842, leaving his family behind, he sailed across the Atlantic Ocean, making his way to Upper Canada and the London area. His search proved positive, and with the help of his friend and fellow Irishman, Jim Hodgins, he sent for Johannah and the child. In 1845, their second son was born in the City of London. Baby William came into the world with a deformed foot. He was later referred to as "Clubfoot Will."

The Donnellys were eager to put down permanent roots. James had learned that many of his countrymen had settled north of London on the Roman Line in Biddulph Township. The area was almost exclusively Irish, and the influx had come mostly from Tipperary. James Donnelly Sr. searched the township, found a section of land on the Roman Line that was uninhabited, and, after learning that the settlement duties had not been paid, the Donnelly family squatted on the 100-acre property. They built a log cabin, cleared the forest, and worked very hard to turn the land into a workable family farm. Between the years of 1847 and 1858, John, Patrick, Michael, Robert, Thomas, and daughter Jane, known as Jenny, were born on the Biddulph Township farm.

Homesteaders in the area resented the fact that the Donnelly family finagled the property without ever paying a single shilling. Things started to go awry in 1855, when the original property owner sold fifty acres of the Donnelly homestead to Michael Maher. James Donnelly was livid and dared anyone to try and take the other fifty acres away from him. No one challenged him, except Patrick Farrell, a fellow Irishman who leased the newly purchased land from Michael Maher.

It was an era of fighting and drunkenness, and James Donnelly and his sons were experts in both fields. There is some speculation that the settlers from Ireland brought their feuding into the New World. Historically, Tipperary, where most of the settlers originated, had a reputation of being the most violent county in Ireland. The murder rate in that county in the nineteenth century was about three times the national average. The Donnelly family certainly exhibited

James Donnelly and his wife Johannah (Magee) Donnelly as they may have looked in their later years.

some of those quarrelsome characteristics, fighting among their neighbours and displaying a quick temper. In fairness, many of the people with whom they quarrelled in Biddulph Township were equally headstrong and quick to pick a fight.

As the settlers from Tipperary established their new homesteads, occurrences of arson, beatings, and drunkenness quickly became the norm. On the 25th of June 1857, Donnelly and Farrell were at William Maloney's logging bee. As was the custom at such gatherings, alcoholic drink was plentiful, and the combination of booze and their hatred for each other resulted in a fight between the two men and the death of Patrick Farrell.

James Donnelly was branded a murderer. When the police constables were sent to the farm to bring him to justice, he had disappeared. James hid in his own woods to escape arrest. At times, he disguised himself in Johannah's clothing in order to help with the farming. If neighbours saw a mysterious woman working in the fields, they said nothing to the authorities. When the cold, icy winter weather became too unbearable for sleeping outdoors, James took shelter in neighbours' stables. The loyal friends who helped him hide risked their freedom by aiding a fugitive. Over all those months, no one ever divulged his secret.

Almost a year after the death of Farrell, the daunting reality of hiding outside for another brutal Canadian winter was too much for James Donnelly. He decided to turn himself in. James did so on the advice of friends, including Justice of the Peace Jim Hodgins. Accompanied by Mitchell Haskett, James turned himself in to Sheriff John McDonald. During the spring trial at Goderich, the defence of intoxication did not stand and James was found guilty. "Death by hanging!" was pronounced by Judge Sir John Beverly Robinson. James was to swing by the neck the following September.

Johannah petitioned for leniency and mercy, gathering signatures for her cause. By July, she was successful in having the sentence changed. Attorney General John A. MacDonald recommended clemency and James began a seven-year sentence in the Provincial Penitentiary of the Province of Canada, now the Kingston Penitentiary. Upon completion of his sentence on the 22nd of July 1865, James returned home to his farm on the Roman Line. Not only did he have sons who were now grown men but also he had a daughter he barely knew. Jane (Jenny), a precocious, pretty child of nine, quickly won her father's heart, and he spoiled her relentlessly.

In May of 1873, the second eldest son, William, started the Donnelly Stagecoach Line, which operated between Lucan and London. John Hawkshaw already ran a successful stagecoach business, and fierce competition ensued between the two. During the fall of that year, Hawkshaw gave up the fight and sold his stage line to Patrick Flanagan and Ted Crowley. Those two entrepreneurs were determined to run the Donnellys into the ground. Competing for passengers was fierce, resulting in a feud between the Donnellys and the new owners. Threats, assaults, and even sabotage were the order of the day. Collisions on the open road were common, disrupting and stressing the paying passengers. Animals were intentionally injured and feuding led to stable fires and late-night mutilations of horses. To guard against break-ins and fires, men were hired to stop or shoot suspicious intruders. It was recorded that James Donnelly Jr. died of natural causes on the 15th of May 1877, but it was thought by many the bullet of a hired firewatcher might have hit him the night before. He was the first of the Donnelly family to be buried in St. Patrick's Church cemetery.

Biddulph Township and the village of Lucan became known as a hostile area, full of rowdy and lawless men. Robert Donnelly was arrested in March of 1878 for the attempted murder of Constable Sam Everett. Judge Wilson changed the sentence to guilty of shooting to do grievous bodily harm, and Robert was received at the Provincial Penitentiary of the Province of Canada, two miles west of Kingston, on the 3rd of April 1878. His sentence ran for two years.

Johannah, living in a house full of men, welcomed her husband's niece Bridget Donnelly with open arms when she came to Canada from Ireland. At the same time, Father John Connolly, a Catholic priest, was transferred to Biddulph from Quebec. It was the hope of the congregation of St. Patrick's Church that Father Connolly would be able to help end the wildness that plagued the area. Their hope proved to be futile. When it was obvious that Father Connolly's suggestions were not working, the possibility of forming a committee of loyal men to help him was considered. Ray Fazakas, in his book *In Search of the Donnellys*, notes that the priest was instrumental in forming the Property Protective Association of St. Patrick's, which later became known as the Vigilance Committee

of Biddulph. Ironically, its members liked to call themselves the Peace Society of Biddulph. The first meeting was held at the Cedar Swamp Schoolhouse on the 7th day of August 1879. Strict rules were formulated and the members were sworn to secrecy. If their intent was keeping the peace, it was single-mindedly focused on the Donnellys.

Just before Christmas of 1879, the Donnelly family suffered another tragedy. James's and Johannah's fifth son, Michael, was stabbed to death during a heated argument in a Waterford hotel. The village of Waterford is located north of Simcoe, Ontario. At the time, Michael was working in St. Thomas on the railroad. The twenty-nine-year-old left a widow and two fatherless children behind. He, too, was buried in St. Patrick's Cemetery.

In January of 1880, Patrick Ryder's barns were torched. Arson was suspected, and the Donnellys were the number one suspects. When it was learned that Will, John, Robert, and Tom had rock-solid alibis, their parents were arrested instead. The trial bogged down when the prosecution could not produce any evidence, and they requested more time to prepare. That one event became the catalyst for the impatient Vigilance Committee to take the law into their own hands. Their intent was to forcefully extract confessions from the Donnellys, hoping to send them to prison.

The day of February 3rd, 1880, started innocently enough for the Donnelly family. Tom and his father, James, made a trip to Lucan for supplies. Driving their horse-drawn wagon back to the farm, they stopped to pick up Johnny O'Connor. The twelve-year-old lad was to stay

**James Donnelly,
his son Tom, niece Bridget,
his wife Johannah, and their son John
were all massacred
by members of the Vigilance Committee.**

overnight, helping with the farm chores the following day while the family attended court in Granton.

Late that evening, under the cover of darkness, about thirty-five men, all members of the Vigilance Committee, made their way along the Roman Line. They were heavily armed with guns, pitchforks, axes, and shovels. Some of the men were disguised as women, some had their faces blackened, some wore dark, heavy coats, and most were fortified with drink.

Once the group reached the Donnelly property, they quietly surrounded the house. Without making a sound, James Carroll made his way inside through the unlocked front door and entered a bedroom directly off the kitchen. As Tom Donnelly slept, Carroll slipped handcuffs

around his wrists. A commotion erupted, waking the entire household. Carroll screamed for help and his accomplices raced into the house, hitting James Sr. over the head, breaking his skull and beating him to death. Tom, his wrists bound in handcuffs, fled for the open door. He was stabbed several times with a pitchfork and dragged back into the house to be killed. Johannah was struck a fatal blow as she tried to crawl away from her attackers. The murderers found Bridget hiding in an upstairs loft. She was killed and her limp body dragged downstairs to lie beside the other corpses. Not even the family dog was spared. Prior to leaving the gruesome scene, the Vigilance Committee set fire to the house.

Unknown to the killers, Johnny O'Connor

had been hiding in an upstairs room under a bed behind a large clothesbasket. The terrified youngster heard and observed much of the massacre. When he no longer heard any noise coming from downstairs, he crawled out from his hiding spot. Exiting the smoke-filled house with flames leaping up the walls, the half-dressed, barefoot Johnny raced through the snow to the neighbouring farm of Patrick Whalen. As he burst into the Whalen home, Johnny blurted out the horrific tale, whilst the Donnelly home burned to the ground.

That same night, not content with killing James Sr., Johannah, Tom, and Bridget, the mob went to the home of Will Donnelly further up the Roman Line at Whalen Corners. Will's brother John had arrived earlier in the evening to pick up a cutter to take the family to court the next day. He had decided to sleep over. As the killers approached Will's home, a couple of them banged on the door yelling out that his house was on fire. Brother John was the first to wake and, as he opened the door, he was shot at close range in the chest, dying instantly. The men fled

the scene believing that they had killed William.

Early the following morning, Johnny O'Connor was taken to his parent's home. He told his father, Michael, what he'd witnessed. Michael O'Connor sent telegrams to Robert and Patrick Donnelly and to Jenny Currie, brothers and sister of the slain. At the same time, the police authorities in London were notified.

On the 6th of February 1880, Father John

"Clubfoot" William, second eldest son of James and Johannah Donnelly, along with twelve-year-old Johnny O'Connor, survived the massacre. Father John Connolly was instrumental in forming a protective association, which later became known as the Vigilance Committee of Biddulph.

Connolly, the organizer of the Vigilance Committee, buried the five Donnellys in St. Patrick's graveyard. Soon after the burial, the London Police made a number of arrests. James Carroll, Martin McLaughlin, John Purtell, and James and Thomas Ryder remained in custody, as did Will Donnelly's brother-in-law John Kennedy. At an inquest, Johnny O'Connor was

Robert Donnelly, his sister Jennie Currie, and brother Patrick, learned of the family tragedy when Michael O'Connor, father of Johnny, sent them telegrams the following morning.

asked to recall the night of February 3rd to 4th. Not only did he tell them what happened, he also named some of the men he had observed that night.

At the close of the trial, the proceedings ended in a hung jury. A second trial concluded with: "The Donnellys were killed by unknown persons"! Inconceivably, no convictions were obtained. Not a single person was found guilty. The jubilant acquitted men returned by stagecoach to Lucan, to a booze-flowing reception hosted by their friends.

One can only imagine the feeling of impotent rage that must have consumed the remaining Donnelly family members. Will Donnelly never gave up hope of bringing the guilty to trial. Over the years, he tenaciously followed any lead, trying to unearth evidence to warrant a new trial. He was convinced

that sooner or later justice would prevail. However, it was not to be earthly justice.

The surviving members of the Donnelly family lived out their lives as honest, respectable citizens. Patrick Donnelly went back to his work and home in Thorold near Niagara Falls, and William ran a hotel in Appin until his death in 1897. From 1901 to 1905, Robert Donnelly and his nephew James Michael Donnelly operated the Western Hotel on William Street in Lucan. In 1911, Robert Donnelly died. Jenny, the only daughter, returned to her Protestant husband James Currie and their twelve children in St. Thomas. She passed away on the 3rd of September 1917, at the age of sixty-one.

Today, Biddulph Township is a prosperous farming community, bearing tribute to the Donnellys' hard-working Irish descendants.

London Police arrested six members of the Vigilance Committee, including left to right, John Purtell, Constable James Carroll, and Martin McLaughlin. No one was ever found guilty.
A second trial concluded with:
"The Donnellys were killed by unknown persons."

Seven Years in Prison

Hatred between James Donnelly Sr. and Patrick Farrell over a land dispute culminated with Farrell's death on the 25th of June 1857. A logging bee on the Roman Line farm of William Maloney was the scene of the murder. After quarrelling, pushing, and shoving, the men became physical towards each other. Picking up a handspike, Donnelly smashed it against Farrell's left temple, dropping him to the ground. Patrick Farrell lay quiet, bleeding. His life ended minutes later.

On the 14th of May 1858, Chief Justice John Beverley Robinson sentenced James Donnelly to death. The death penalty for the father of eight was commuted to seven years in the Provincial Penitentiary of the Province of Canada, now called the Kingston Penitentiary.

In February 2005, I visited Canada's Penitentiary Museum in Kingston. I spoke with curator David St. Onge in his office on the second floor of the warden's old home with windows overlooking the Kingston Penitentiary across the street. St. Onge explained that the original ledger books, with Donnelly's records, are now stored for safekeeping in the National Archives in Ottawa. He went on to describe how James Donnelly would have been received at the prison on the 6th of August 1858.

"James Donnelly Sr. would have arrived here in the village of Portsmouth, either by stagecoach or train," said St. Onge. "He would have been brought through the front gates in shackles. Inmates were entered numerically in the entry book, and Donnelly was assigned #4615. After the shackles were removed, Donnelly would be taken to the bathhouse to be shaved and scrubbed. If necessary, he would be deloused. He was given his inmate's uniform with #4615 stitched to the fabric. In August, he would have received a summer uniform made of denim. Called the party coloured uniform, it consisted of trousers with one black and one white leg. The jacket and waistcoat would be split into black and white as well. Only prisoners in the United States wore black and white stripes. During the winter months, the denim was replaced with a warmer wool uniform. One half was dark brown and the other half yellow."

Curator St. Onge escorted me to a cell in another part of the museum to show me that by today's standards, they had few luxuries. The cells were tiny, measuring twenty-nine inches wide by eight feet long. From floor to ceiling, they measured six feet, seven inches in height.

"After having the rules read to him," said St. Onge, "James Donnelly was taken to cell #21 on the first tier of the east wing. A few days after his arrival, he'd get a visit from the penitentiary chaplain. Then it was time to assign Donnelly his forced labour duties. In the mid-1800s, exercise

JAMES DONNELLY SR.

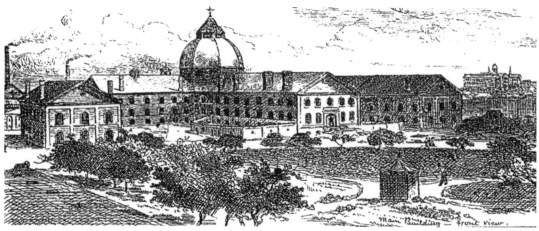

David St. Onge, curator of Canada's Penitentiary Museum, peruses an 1800s ledger book in his office. The Provincial Penitentiary of the Province of Canada, shown in the illustration above, is now called the Kingston Penitentiary.

yards did not exist. The administration felt hard labour was adequate exercise. The prison housed a cabinet factory and shoe factory, a limestone quarry and a stonecutting shop. A tailor shop turned out uniforms not only for the inmates, but for other government agencies as well. There was a sizable farm, which was built up throughout the nineteenth century. In the 1850s–'60s, the land consisted of an original 100-acre parcel purchased in 1833. By the 1890s, it was 300 acres in total. Donnelly may have worked on the farm or in one of the industrial shops. During the first year of his incarceration, he may have helped to build the dome in the centre of the penitentiary. As a labourer he would have worked from sunrise to sunset."

David St. Onge went on to say: "From the 21st of February until the 2nd of March 1863, Donnelly was hospitalized for contusions. This may have been a job-related injury."

During his seven years of incarceration, the five-foot, four-inch Irish farm labourer was written up in the *Punishment Register* seven times.

#4615 – JAMES DONNELLY

16 July 1859 For talking at (his) work.
 Punishment = 3 meals bread & water
28 Nov. 1859 For talking & complaining at (his) work.
 Punishment = 6 meals bread & water, 2 nights without bed.
19 Feb. 1860 For not using clean shirt which was left in his cell, also for having a vest made from a blanket.
 Punishment = 3 meals bread & water

9 Mar. 1860 For taking bread & meat from dining hall.
 Punishment = 4 meals bread & water
14 Mar. 1860 For talking at breakfast table.
 Punishment = 4 meals bread & water, 1 night without bed.
18 Jan. 1862 For laughing & talking to Teamster in yard.
 Punishment = 5 meals bread & water
27 Sept. 1864 For quarrelling while working with fellow convicts & refusing to go back to work.
 Punishment = 6 meals bread & water, 2 nights without bed.

The practice of interviewing convicts who were completing their sentences began August 8th, 1836. The questions were designed to assist administrators in determining if there were weaknesses in security or mistreatment of convicts by guards. They also hoped to receive some feedback from departing convicts about their reaction to various punishments; the accommodations provided in the penitentiary for heating and cell size; and how the convicts would compare the penitentiary to the common gaol. The following *Liberation Questions* were put to James Donnelly Sr. on the 22nd of July 1865. The answers are quoted in italics as recorded by the scribe.

1. How long have you been a prisoner in the Penitentiary?
 Since the sixth day of August, 1858.
2. Have you suffered any, and if so, what punishments during your imprisonment?
 Has not had any punishment.

3. Have you ever seen any cruel treatment inflicted upon prisoners, and what is your opinion generally upon the manner in which the convicts are treated?

Has not, nor half so much as many of them deserved. He has found himself well treated.

4. Have you found the cells and other portions of the Institution sufficiently heated and ventilated?

Has found them so.

5. Are the cells sufficiently large?

They are small enough.

6. Is the food of the Prisoners sufficient and of good quality?

He was satisfied, and considered it good.

7. Are the clothing and bedding sufficient and suitable for the various seasons?

It is.

8. Are the sick prisoners treated with attention and humanity?

They are well treated and Mr. Whyman, who is dead and gone, underwent great fatigue and was very kind to him as well as many others.

9. Is the conduct of the Officers and others employed in the Institution humane and kind towards the prisoners?

Never say anything else. He has found them kind to himself.

10. Do you think that under all circumstances, things go on as well as possible in the Penitentiary?

Thinks they do.

11. What do you think is the greatest privation that prisoners are subjected to in the Penitentiary?

The confinement to the cells on Sundays.

12. Do you think the system adopted in the Institution together with the religious instruction tends to reform the prisoners and is sufficient to attain that end?

Thinks every trouble and pains are taken with them and in many cases without effect.

13. Do you think that the fear of confinement in prison or in the Penitentiary is sufficient to deter from crime?

Cannot say. He never heard about the like before his misfortune. Dreaded his God more than earthly punishment.

14. What kind of punishment is, in your opinion, most efficient in maintaining the discipline of the Institution?

Thinks the chain.

15. Have you seen or heard prisoners manifest feelings of revenge against the Officers or others employed in this Institution?

Has heard the like and very wrongfully.

16. What effect does the prospect of being pardoned produce on the prisoners?

Thinks a good effect.

17. What effect does the presence of visitors produce on the prisoners?

It often tried his feelings as well as those of other convicts.

18. Do the prisoners hold conversation among themselves, and where is the most convenient place for conversing without being discovered?

They do when they get the chance. Has never heard men talk in other places than the Roman Catholic Chapel.

19. Had you any knowledge during your imprisonment of any plots being formed among the prisoners?

None to his knowledge.

20. Have you at any time heard news from persons outside and from what sources do prisoners generally receive such information?

None, but from the Warden, from his own family. Has heard many stories but is not aware how information is had.

21. Did you receive a good religious education when you were a child?

He merely was instructed in his religion by his parish priest.

22. How did you obtain your livelihood before being sent to the Penitentiary, and what do you propose doing after you are liberated?

By hard farm labour—will return to his farm labour.

23. What has been the general cause of your misfortunes and what has been the immediate cause of the crime for which you have been sent to the Penitentiary?

Liquors and passion. For killing a man, but merely the effect of passion.

24. In what prison were you confined before coming to the Penitentiary and what would be the probable effect of confinement in that prison on the morals of the prisoners there confined?

In the gaol at Goderich. The effect was very serious in reflecting on his unfortunate crime.

25. How often have you conversed with . your clergyman in the Penitentiary on religious subjects, and during the time of your confinement have you made any progress in your religious instructions?

Twice every year–not more than he had before he came.

26. What is in your opinion the best means of reforming criminals?

Cannot say.

27. Do you think that your imprisonment in the Penitentiary has been beneficial to you in a moral and religious point of view and that you are better qualified to earn a livelihood now than before you entered the Institution?

Not more so than before he came here. Is not so well qualified as before he came here, being further advanced in years.

While researching this material, it became clear to me that James Donnelly had few visitors during his stay in prison and it is doubtful that any of his family made the approximately five-hundred-mile round trip. James was illiterate, and any correspondence that came his way would have been read to him by the warden. On the 22nd day of July 1865, he marked the *Liberation Question Book* with an "X," witnessed by Warden D.A.E. MacDonnell, and J.B. Couillard.

Six days later, on the 28th day of July 1865, James Donnelly was discharged and left the Provincial Penitentiary of the Province of Canada for his home in Lucan.

My Great-Great-Grandparents were Donnellys

As I was researching the Donnelly family, I realized that I had yet to come across a present-day Donnelly descendant. I was still pondering this lack of information when I received a telephone call from my friend Tim Gordon, publisher at General Store Publishing House in Renfrew, Ontario. "Terry, did you know that a Donnelly descendant lives in Ottawa? His house burned down on Christmas Day, 2004. The *Ottawa Citizen* profiled this story on the 125th anniversary of the Donnelly massacre," Tim said.

After a couple of calls, I was able to contact Richard Egan, a fifty-eight-year-old Ottawa lawyer and owner of the home on Fifth Avenue in the Glebe District that had burned to the ground. Richard graciously agreed to talk to me at his office.

Richard traces his lineage back through James and Johannah Donnelly, who had seven sons and a daughter called Jane, better known as Jenny. Jenny married James Currie on the 9th of February 1874 in Bothwell, Ontario. They produced a total of twelve children. Their fifth child, Jane, was born on March 12th, 1886. Jane would become Richard Egan's grandmother. Jane Currie married Michael Egan and they settled in Windsor, Ontario, where Mike worked

as a conductor on the railroad, a very prestigious position at the time. "I remember being fascinated by pictures of my grandmother Jane taken about the time she married. She was an extremely beautiful woman and I would like to have learned more about her as a young person. Unfortunately, we never talked much about our family history. We were encouraged to look forward, not backward.

"I always knew that my grandmother had a very strong faith. As a practising Catholic, she had a little upholstered prayer stool in her living room, one of the many items that held a great fascination for me. Every weekend, the entire family would visit Grandma's house. It was a family ritual. All of us would be gathered around her lush, red Victorian sofa, chatting and laughing. I remember sitting on the floor at the end of that sofa, playing with two little elephant knick-knacks while Grandma was watching the boxing matches on the *Gillette Cavalcade of Sports*, one of her favourite shows.

"My grandparents had three sons, Tom, Jack, and Jim, my father. Jack never married, but Tom did and had two sons, Wayne and Tommy, and one daughter named Jane. All of us fondly remember the good times around that beautiful

Ottawa lawyer Richard Egan is a direct descendant of James and Johannah Donnelly. His great-grandmother was Jenny (Donnelly) Currie, James and Johannah's only daughter.

ethics and values. They never wavered from their ethical code and lived their entire life true to those values. I have never been able to get a handle on this, but suspect that it links back to the Donnelly massacre.

"I have always known that I was of Irish background, but as a child was never told of our Donnelly connection. I suspect that my parents wanted to spare me schoolyard bullying and I'm thankful for that. I didn't find out that I was a descendant until the late 1970s. I was at my Grandmother Jane's funeral in Windsor. Friends and relatives came from the London area, and we were all having a meal at my Uncle Tom's home. One of the visitors innocently remarked: 'Oh, you have to watch out for the Donnellys!' Someone else in the room piped up: 'We are the Donnellys!' It came as a shock and surprise to me."

That revelation prompted Richard to read anything and everything about his ancestry. He decided to visit Lucan. "I was quite convinced that I'd never find the Donnelly property and I'd also heard that the original tombstone had been removed. I didn't have much to go by; I never even ventured down the Roman Line. All I

old velvet sofa. When I inherited the chesterfield as part of uncle Jack's estate, I was thrilled because it brought back those wonderful memories. Unfortunately, my spouse did not share my attachment and I was forced to dispose of that lovely old piece of furniture.

"It was only after the death of Uncle Jack that I began to realize how very strong my grandparents' faith was. As the beneficiary, I had to go through the house and I found rosaries, crucifixes, and glass candlesticks in the shape of crucifixes. Pictures of the Virgin Mary and The Sacred Heart were everywhere. The two redeeming qualities I can pass on in regard to my grandparents are that one, they had a strong Catholic faith, and two, they had very strong

QUEENS HOTEL

CENTRAL HOTEL

Terry Culbert's Lucan ~ Home of the Donnellys

wanted to see was this damn saloon, called the Queens Hotel, apparently the favourite watering hole of the Donnellys. The only hotel I could find was the Central Hotel on Main Street. I didn't even go in for a drink," Richard said. At the time of Richard's visit, the Central Hotel was the only operational beverage room in the village. The Queens, Royal, Dominion, Western, and Fitzhenry Hotels, along with the Revere and Dublin Houses, had closed many, many years earlier. My research shows that the staunch Protestant Robert McLean, Central Hotel tavern keeper at the time of the Donnellys, frowned on Catholic patrons.

When asked about his feelings regarding the Donnelly feud, Richard explained: "I feel strongly that the primary reason for feuding with the Donnellys was land ownership, remembering they were squatters on someone else's property. One has to also keep in mind that the rail line was foremost in everyone's thoughts at that time. The little town of Lucan was important in that the rail lines ran through it to ship local farmers' goods across the land and, in turn, provide the farmers with seeds and supplies. Property ownership meant possible future rail line profits. People were speculating where tracks would be laid and whose land would be affected. The Donnellys, being in the stagecoach business, would have had a vested interest in the rail lines. I have always felt that the property issue is an essential part to understanding the Donnelly saga."

Richard was born in May of 1947 in Windsor to Doris and James Egan. They moved to Brockville when he was ten years of age. As a young man, he attended the University of Guelph, receiving a degree in English and Philosophy. He met and began living common-law with Susan Weiss. They resided in Guelph for quite a few years. "I became an inside postal worker, ending up with a strong union bent," said Richard. "I assisted in reorganizing the union local, which was exciting and piqued my interest in labour issues. I decided to go back to school and learn more about labour arbitration and labour relations. I attended the University of Windsor, obtaining a law degree. Here I am today in Ottawa as a sole practitioner in family law, the other end of the spectrum from where I originally wanted to be."

Richard's daughter Kelly Egan, the sixth generation of the family, proudly traces her roots back to James Donnelly, the Irish patriarch of the Donnelly clan from Borrisokane, Tipperary, Ireland. The Toronto filmmaker is presently enrolled in a PhD program and plans to one day produce a film of her family's story.

Biddulph Vigilance Committee Descendant

In the early 1990s, I produced a television profile on William Ryder of London, Ontario. William's great-uncles were Patrick "Grouchy," James "Sideroad," and Thomas "Pitchfork" Ryder, brothers of William's great-grandfather John Ryder. William's father was raised on the infamous Roman Line south of Lucan. Ryder was in his thirties when I did the story on his quest to open a Donnelly Museum in his hometown of London. The Grosvenor Lodge in the northwest part of the city was to be the site. His hard work and dreams were dashed, as the City of London had other plans for the empty building. The part-time historian pressed on, writing a screenplay with the working title: *Forgive Us Our Trespassers*. The dialogue is based on newspaper accounts and court trial transcripts.

"My interest in the Donnellys began when I was in my early teens," said William. "In Grade 10 at Catholic Central High School, the teacher gave our class an assignment to recount something fascinating about our individual family history. I have always considered my family tree exciting because of our huge connection to the tragedy of the Donnelly family in Biddulph. The more I researched my family history, the more my interest grew, and the assignment was completed in no time."

William's interest in the Donnellys also spilled over into art. He is a talented artist who paints, sculpts, and creates three-dimensional works. His first show was held at the Myriad Gallery across from the Covent Garden Market in London, Ontario. Twenty-seven years of age at the time, William displayed three dozen Donnelly-related pieces in his one-man show. "The greatest compliment I received was from a biker dressed in his leathers and chains. I walked up to him and asked if he was enjoying the show. His response: 'It's some scary shit, man!' I felt I'd really arrived as an artist to be able to evoke such strong emotion from a tough-looking biker," smiled Ryder.

In 2001, Ryder was invited to Lucan to show his art at the Ausable Community Centre. It was the 121st anniversary of the Donnelly massacre. "I was well received in Lucan and within twenty minutes of the show's opening, a woman purchased one of my paintings. She promptly donated it to the Lucan Heritage Museum," he recalls. "The show ran for almost a month and sparked a lot of interest. I would love to become involved with the new Lucan

Museum. I feel I contributed a great deal in bringing the Donnelly story to the forefront," said Ryder. "After all these long years of silence, people are now starting to talk about Lucan's notorious past. Even relatives on my father's side are suddenly eager to explore their history."

Artist William Ryder's great uncles were Patrick "Grouchy," James "Sideroad," and Thomas "Pitchfork," all brothers of William's great-grandfather John Ryder.

Dinner with Johnny O'Connor

Meeting Johnny O'Connor, the only person to survive the Donnelly massacre of February 4th, 1880, would make an impression on most people. For William Kilmer, son of Clandeboye farmers Louis and Connie Kilmer, it has been a lasting memory since 1934. "I grew up with the Donnelly stories and it was a thrill at the age of ten to meet the legendary O'Connor," Kilmer said. The memorable event happened during a visit with his parents to family friends in Toledo, Ohio. At the home of William Bernard Hodgins and his niece Lina Huggins, young Kilmer was introduced to a man sitting in their living room. "I don't think he used his real name, but it was similar, something like Cochrane or Conners," William recalls. "I remember him being a shy, lean man with graying hair. He stood about five feet eight inches in height and was sixty-eight years of age. He seemed in good physical shape."

Jeremiah (Johnny) O'Connor was born in Biddulph Township. He was the son of Michael and Mary Hastings O'Connor. On the afternoon of February 3rd, 1880, James Donnelly and his son Tom picked up the young lad from his parents' home, bringing him to their farm to stay overnight. That night, young O'Connor would witness the heinous murder by the Vigilance Committee of Biddulph of James and Johannah, their son Tom, and niece Bridget Donnelly, who was visiting from Ireland.

During the months that followed, Johnny was an important witness at the inquest of those accused. At a preliminary hearing, enough evidence was put forth to hold an actual trial. The Crown attorney moved the O'Connor family from Lucan to London for their protection. With that, the Donnelly trial finally began in October of 1880. Key testimony for the prosecution came from William Donnelly and Johnny O'Connor. Not one, but two trials later, the jury found Constable James Carroll and the other defendants not guilty of the Donnelly murders, and they were released from the London jail.

Records show Johnny O'Connor, at the age of twenty, working for McClary Stoves in London. He also worked as a labourer with a London firm called Hymans. At some point, Johnny disappeared from the area, and no records exist. He eventually resurfaced in Toledo, Ohio.

William Kilmer and his family visited their Toledo friends twice in 1934. And twice, Johnny O'Connor was a dinner guest. According to Kilmer, during his second visit, Johnny seemed relaxed and talkative. "I remember O'Connor as being soft-spoken," said Kilmer, "and it was at that last visit that I heard him speak about the Donnelly murders. I remember him talking about Buckshot Ryder as one of the Vigilantes. Even

In 1934, William Kilmer, pictured on the left, met Johnny O'Connor. William was ten at the time. Johnny, pictured in the author's drawing, was sixty-eight years of age and lived in the United States.

though I was young and impressionable, to my great surprise, O'Connor insisted that the parish priest was among the group that night. There was no doubt in O'Connor's mind that Father John Connolly was present at the massacre of the Donnelly family on the 4th of February 1880."

Apparently, O'Connor did not repeat that dire allegation in later years, and no one else ever implicated Father Connelly. However, there were rumours that the priest had been aware that members of the Vigilance Committee, which he had formed, intended to take the law into their own hands. It was also known that the priest had openly denounced the Donnelly family at his church.

One had to wonder if Johnny O'Connor's accusations were the result of a young boy in shock, or if indeed there was involvement by the local priest, if only by quietly condoning the actions of his parishioners.

There is no School Today

Eliza O'Keefe would never forget the morning of February 4th, 1880. That was the day her teacher stood outside the Donnelly School on the Roman Line and uttered the words: "There won't be any school today. The Donnellys were all killed last night!" It was the morning after James, Johannah, Tom, John, and Bridget Donnelly were massacred by the Vigilance Committee. An impressionable young Eliza O'Keefe would one day relate the story of the tragedy to her daughter, Mary Mitchell.

Mary (Mitchell) Whelihan was born on the 20th of January 1914 on Lot 28, Concession 9, known as the Swamp Line. She and her older brother Francis Patrick were the children of Joseph Mitchell and Eliza O'Keefe. Mary's grandfather Robert O'Keefe had pioneered the land next to her parents after emigrating from County Kerry, Ireland. The land was still in the O'Keefe name, operated by Robert and Rose O'Keefe, the unmarried brother and sister of Mary's mother Eliza.

Mary recalls her Aunt Rose and Uncle Bob entertaining a special visitor one summer. It was their long-time friend Norah Donnelly. Norah was the widow of William Donnelly, the second eldest son of James and Johannah, who were so brutally murdered in 1880. William had been a horseman and hotelkeeper before he died in 1897 at the age of fifty-two.

Norah had brought her grandchildren Ione and Jack Clay from London to the country for a holiday. Ione, Jack, and Mary became instant friends, and at least twice a day the trio would cut across the fields, squeezing through an opening in the line-fence, to play tag with each other.

"I remember Norah Donnelly as a big-framed, well-built, tall woman," said Mary. "She was a distinguished-looking lady who talked with a very loud voice, but was kind and always eager to help. One day, while they were visiting, my Uncle Bob was busy thrashing and it was up to Aunt Rose to bring in the cows. It was not unusual in those days for women to tie up the cows and do the milking. Mrs. Donnelly offered to give Aunt Rose a hand. She found a milking stool and proceeded to milk one of the cows. That particular cow was not too happy about this turn of events and administered a well-placed kick, knocking Norah off her milking stool. Norah's fall was so hard that she broke her wrist. In those days, X-rays did not exist. Doctor Mitton in Granton took one look at her wrist, bandaged it up, and sent Norah back to the farm in the horse and buggy she came in.

"Over the years, I met up with Mrs. Donnelly a few times. The last time was in 1937 at St. Joseph's Hospital, where she was admitted with a terminal illness. I was a nurse at the

The Donnelly schoolhouse was erected in 1878.

Photo courtesy of Ray Fazakas.

hospital and when I saw her name, I decided to go and visit her. Norah Donnelly did not recognize me—she was dying and was long past knowing people!"

Mary fondly recalls her years in the Donnelly one-room schoolhouse. "Less than twenty pupils attended the school. Toilet facilities consisted of an outhouse in the schoolyard, and with no well on the property, water was supplied in pails from nearby farms. I remember very clearly at the age of seven, developing diphtheria. I was the first person in Middlesex County to get an anti-toxin serum. Even though I was a very sick little girl, somehow that dubious honour made me feel quite special," smiled Mary.

"Life was hard on the farm, and everyone pitched in to help. We did not have electricity

until 1951. Cows were milked by hand and there were no cream separators. We used flat pans and crocks to collect the milk, storing it in our cool cellar. The meat was cured, salted, and dried. Washing was done on a scrub board; it was a long, drawn-out process and could take days. Looking after a household was a full-time job. We didn't have any of the conveniences that people take for granted nowadays. Of course, you can't miss what you've never had or never experienced.

"My parents did not have a car. I actually helped buy the first tractor after finishing nurses' training. It was a godsend and helped the men greatly with their daily work. Things did not always turn out for the better, though. I never forgot one hot afternoon. The men were using the binder, bringing in horses for their daily feeding. I noticed that one horse was sweating profusely and it did look as though it was in distress. I quickly grabbed a pail of cold water and threw it over the horse's head, hoping to cool it down with my action. To my horror, the horse stumbled, fell to the ground and died. I was devastated. What I thought was the correct thing to do had turned into a disaster. The men had trouble removing the horse from the team, as the dead the animal was stuck in the middle. It was a horrible experience," Mary recalled.

"But we had many happy times, too. Christmas was my favourite. Food played a large role; it was plentiful and delicious. I fondly remember Christmas dinner. We always served a large turkey with all the trimmings. What a feast."

Mary Mitchell graduated from the St. Joseph School of Nursing in 1934. She married Joseph Michael Robert Whelihan, a farmer from Whalen Corners. A son, Patrick Joseph, was born in 1950. After graduating from the University of Western Ontario, Patrick became a high school teacher in Chatham. When Mary and Joe retired from the farm, they moved to the village of Lucan. After four decades of marriage, Mary became a widow.

Mary (Mitchell) Whelihan in her Lucan home during the spring of 2003.

Norah, widow of William Donnelly, was a close friend of Mary (Mitchell) Whelihan's family.

The Birth of the Donnelly Museum

The International Council of Museums defines a museum as a place that exhibits and communicates the evidence of people and their environment for the purpose of study, education, and enjoyment.

Not many villages, towns, or cities have a history of people and their environment as important and varied as the southwestern Ontario village of Lucan. For example, the Wilberforce Settlement, the community built by free blacks from the United States in 1829, and the infamous Donnelly saga are important Canadian historical events that took place in the Lucan area. Why, then, has it taken until 1995 to start a museum in Lucan Biddulph? I suspect there has always been a fear of upsetting families and relatives who may have had a connection to the feuding and the massacre of the Donnelly family in 1880. The Donnelly tragedy was not mentioned for many years, and if at all, it was spoken in whispers. I can attest to this, having grown up in the village. I have a deep respect for the townspeople of Lucan, especially the core group that had the courage and foresight to bring the historic Donnelly story into the open. They have lifted the burden of shame and have instilled pride into their community.

The Lucan Area Heritage Society was formed in April of 1995. Having gathered enough historical artifacts, their first display was set up in an old Ford dealership showroom on Lucan's Main Street. Determined to one day exhibit in their own building, the non-profit organization was faced with the enormous task of raising money. The first large fundraiser was a Cash Calendar, with a prize drawn every day of the year. This popular event netted the Society $25,000 within two years and is now produced annually.

With the fundraising proceeds, the Heritage Society was able to purchase a village lot on Frank Street, which included a two-car garage, to be refurbished as a museum building. In 1998, the society bought, transported, and reconstructed an original early-1800s log cabin from Bruce County. A barn was donated to the Society by Mrs. Kit Hearn, which originally was used by her husband, Ivan, to house his horses and milk wagons for their dairy. Delighted with their progress, the society nevertheless was in desperate need of a museum building to meet the standards for preserving historical artefacts set by the Federal Ministry of Culture.

When the Lucan Lions Club heard of their plight, they purchased the vacant property on which the Central Hotel (circa 1846) once stood. The hotel was destroyed by fire on the 11th of January 1995. The Lions Club has agreed to transfer ownership of the land to the Township of Lucan Biddulph for the future use of the

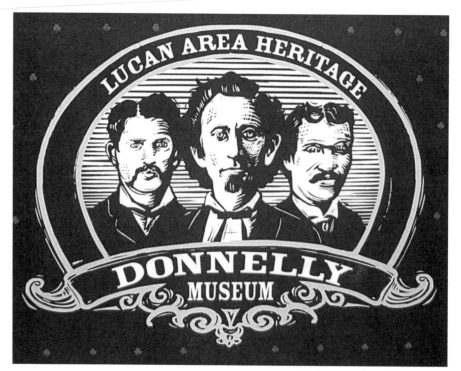

The Lucan Area Heritage Donnelly Museum logo.

**Sheila Hodgins, Jean Hodgins, Jackie Martens, and Muriel Culbert
are all members of the Lucan Area Heritage Society.**

x

Lucan Area Heritage Donnelly Museum.

On the site, a proposed 12,000-square-foot building will be erected, with its front doors facing Main Street. The museum will replicate the old Central Hotel, including a second-floor balcony. The structure will be environmentally controlled and will have a basement. The estimated cost for the completed museum will be close to one million dollars.

By the spring of 2005, the society had reached their halfway goal. "Trying to raise money for such a large project from a small population base and maintain interest is difficult," claims Sheila Hodgins, the society secretary. "We have persevered so far and will not let up with our fundraising projects."

Innovative fundraisers include the annual February Heritage Dinner, the Awesome Auction, Heritage Day, the Christmas Home Tour, and a bus tour organized to retrace the Vigilantes' route. Over 400 visitors rode the buses on the evening of February 3rd, 2005, the 125th anniversary of the Donnelly massacre.

The following editorial was written by Brad Harness, editor of *The Middlesex Banner*, in February 2005.

When I first came to Lucan, folks were too inward-looking to give serious consideration to leveraging the national prominence of the Donnelly tragedy for

Painting by Jan Brouwer

An early 1800s reconstructed log cabin purchased by the Heritage Society in Bruce County.

local economic gain. After seeing dozens of new businesses try and fail, largely due to poor planning and little in the way of creativity and market research, pinning Lucan's tail on the Donnelly donkey means we will move forward at last. Yes, it was a tragic event, but it is the approximation of the Americans' "Shootout at the O.K. Corral" that we have here. The Yanks like it, Canadians find it compelling, so why not give the people what they want? Avoid the tacky trinkets, but go for this brass ring like there's no tomorrow. Most folks don't work locally or need to. But for those who do, this promises to be a regular Bonanza if it is done right. Let's hope that it is, and keep donating to the Museum Fund to make it a reality.

Theatrical Donnelly Trial

The Donnelly Trial, a new play by documentary maker and playwright Christopher Doty, was first held at a public reading on March 3rd, 2005, in the London Public Library's Wolf Performance Hall. The audience was mesmerized, listening to professional actors read the lines of William Donnelly, Johnny O'Connor, and the accused constable, James Carroll. The following June, two special performances were held to sold-out audiences in Lucan. By month's end, the three-hour production began a three-week run staged at the former London and Middlesex Court House, now the administrative seat for the County of Middlesex. The county administrators graciously allowed Doty and his cast to use the council chamber that originally housed the actual courtroom used in the trials of 1880 and the winter of 1881. With the exception of the addition of a portrait of Queen Victoria and one of the then premier of Ontario, Oliver Mowat, the room has remained exactly as it was over a century earlier.

What inspired Christopher Doty to turn the Donnelly massacre into a theatrical production? "It occurred to me that most people have heard about the Donnellys," explained Doty, "but don't know any of the details. No one seems to know what exactly happened; there are a lot of unanswered questions. To my mind, this family drama lends itself perfectly to the theatre. I decided not to get my material from the reigning Donnelly writers, but to start fresh. I dug up old newspaper transcripts. There were two trials. The first ended with a hung jury and the second in an acquittal. The *London Advertiser,* the *Toronto Globe,* and the *Toronto Mail* covered the reportage. Throughout my research, I received many suggestions and much well-meaning advice. Some wanted to have ghosts of the Donnellys as part of the play. Others felt I should include a re-enactment of the massacre. After many long and fruitful discussions with my director, Jeff Culbert, who is a fifth-generation Lucanite, I began to understand that the audience would be expecting to see a re-enactment of the original court case. I billed the play as an experience because it is the closest you can get to reliving the Donnelly trial."

Christopher Doty clearly understood the attraction of this part of Canadian history. His play quickly sold out its three-week run in London, Ontario.

The following portion of *The Donnelly Trial* depicts Johnny O'Connor, the fourteen-year-old survivor of the massacre, being cross-examined by defence lawyer William Ralph Meredith. The questions were put in a strong, though perhaps not loud, tone of voice, but were poured on with such rapidity that the boy barely had time to sandwich his answers in between them, allowing not a second for hesitancy or deliberation.

Meredith: *You claim that you saw the murders from under old man Donnelly's bed. Correct?*

O'Connor: *Yes, sir.*

Meredith: *Wasn't there a clothesbasket under the bed as well?*

O'Connor: *Yes. A long willow clothesbasket.*

Meredith: *Wouldn't that have blocked your view?*

O'Connor: *There was about a half a foot space between the basket and the railing of the bed. I could only see their feet when I looked over the top.*

Meredith: *Only their feet?*

O'Connor: *Yes, sir.*

Meredith: *Well, how can you be sure it was Tom Donnelly that was being beaten if you only saw his feet?*

O'Connor: *I saw stocking feet. What would the other men want to be out in their stocking feet for?*

Meredith: *Why did you mention James Carroll's name to Mrs. Whalen?*

O'Connor: *I just thought I should.*

Meredith: *Why? Did you believe Carroll was guilty?*

O'Connor: *Yes, and I wanted Carroll punished for it.*

Playwright Chris Doty stands in front of the old London Middlesex Court House.

Constable James Carroll was accused of murdering Johannah Donnelly.

This is the actual courtroom used in the trials of James Carroll in 1880 and the winter of 1881.

On the evening of Wednesday, June 29th, 2005, I had the pleasure of seeing the play first-hand with my sister Dana and brother-in-law Jack Garrett. Seated next to me was Noel Gallagher, the Arts and Entertainment reporter for the *London Free Press*. The following is a portion of his review:

VERDICT POSITIVE
IN DONNELLY TRIAL

A unique group of circumstances conspires to make *The Donnelly Trial* an engrossing, even haunting, theatre experience. Though no one was ever convicted of the murders, Lucan constable James Carroll was charged with the slaying of Johannah Donnelly, matriarch of the controversial clan, who had feuded with their neighbours and local authorities for decades.

Newspaper accounts and court transcripts from Carroll's trials provide a solid, factual basis for the drama written and produced by Christopher Doty. Heightening the aura of authenticity, director Jeff Culbert and his cast present the story in an honest, straightforward manner, without indulging in unnecessary theatrics. During Wednesday night's sold-out performance, 130 spectators sat transfixed in near-reverent silence as a parade of witnesses gave their contrasting versions of events that occurred on that fateful February night 125 years ago.

At each performance, the ultimate judgment of the case is rendered by a dozen audience members occupying the jury box. In a surprising turn, Wednesday's group rendered a "not guilty" decision for Carroll (Sean Carmichael), who had drawn the death sentence in the show's three previous outings.

As they filed out of the courtroom, the spectators engaged in spirited discussions about the issues raised during this so-real courtroom drama.

Noel Gallagher and I agreed that it was a first-class performance. He gave his review four out of five stars.

The day before I attended the play, I visited Tom McLaughlin, warden of Middlesex County and mayor of Lucan Biddulph. I was in awe as Tom walked me through the doorway into the empty courtroom. This space had not been modernized over the years, albeit the light fixtures are now electric. At the east end of the room, Tom led me into his magnificent office, the former judge's chambers. "This is precisely where the two Donnelly trials took place," Tom said. "The judge would have used this very room. The court constable would inform the judge that the court was to begin and his lordship would take his place behind the bench. Having the play re-enacted in this very courtroom seems almost surreal."

Tom McLaughlin grew up as a farm boy on the Roman Line. His great-uncle was Martin McLaughlin, a member of the Biddulph Vigilance Committee. "There were several mentions of my great-uncle in the play. The mention of his name made me wince a little each time I heard it. Martin McLaughlin was the chairman of the committee and was one of the accused, although he never went on trial. William Donnelly testified he had heard Martin McLaughlin's voice outside his Whalen Corners home the night his brother John was murdered. This of course concerned me a lot upon hearing the story. I hope my great-uncle was not guilty, but if he was, he should have paid the price.

"During the actual trial 125 years ago, Martin's daughter testified that he was at home on the farm that night. My family hardly ever talked about the tragedy, but it was always believed that Martin was away from the area visiting a neighbouring community at the time the killings occurred. John McLaughlin, Martin's brother, was also a member of the Biddulph Vigilance Committee. William, another brother and my great-grandfather, was not involved. I feel the play was very realistic and the acting was superb. It is a credit to playwright Chris Doty and director Jeff Culbert for being able to condense two trials into a three-hour production."

Hopefully *The Donnelly Trial* will be resurrected on an annual basis in the wonderful venue, the old London and Middlesex Courthouse.

Donnelly Documentary

A documentary crew from Western Canada travelled east, visiting the Lucan area three times during 2004–05. Regina, Saskatchewan-based Partners in Motion, a film and video production company, is producing a documentary called *The Donnellys: A Conspiracy of Silence.* Chris Triffo, the president of Partners in Motion, is the director on this project. Set against a backdrop of pioneer life in Upper Canada, it is a true story of violence, love, hatred, revenge, and murder. The story of the Donnellys will be brought to life by a modern investigation recreated by retired Toronto Police Deputy Chief Mike Boyd. As one of Canada's most experienced homicide detectives, Boyd brought innovative science and technology to the courtroom. Treating the Donnelly murders as a cold case, Boyd will work alongside Donnelly author, retired lawyer Ray Fazakas, attempting to reconstruct the events and find out what really occurred that fateful night. Using modern ballistic testing, biomechanical engineering, and scientific content analysis, the case will be examined deeper than ever before.

While in southwestern Ontario, the Partners in Motion crew interviewed Lucan Biddulph Mayor Tom McLaughlin, Robert Salts, owner of the Donnelly homestead on the Roman Line, and Sheila Hodgins of the Lucan Area Heritage Society. They also visited William Kilmer at his

Photos courtesy of Partners in Motion

A scene from the documentary
The Donnellys:
A Conspiracy of Silence,
by Regina-based
Partners in Motion.

Chris Triffo is not only president of the company, but he is also the documentary director. Chris is seen holding an antique pocket watch that once belonged to William Donnelly.

home near the hamlet of St. Joseph on Lake Huron. As a lad of ten, Kilmer met the legendary sixty-eight-year-old Johnny O'Connor, the lone survivor of the Donnelly massacre. Partners in Motion's one-hour documentary *The Donnellys: A Conspiracy of Silence* is still in production and when complete will be broadcast nationally on History Television. For up-to-date information visit: **www.partnersinmotion.com**

Grouchy Ryder's Farm

In 1957, Peggy and Barney Rooney decided to relinquish teaching school in Belfast, Northern Ireland, for an unknown future in faraway Canada. After packing up their belongings, the Rooneys immigrated to Canada with their children, Hugh and Joyce. They settled in London, Ontario, where Barney found work with the Catholic Board of Education as a teacher, then as a principal, eventually winding up his career teaching history at Catholic Central High School in London. Joyce made the daily trek into the country to teach Grade 8 and special education at St. Patrick's Catholic School on the Roman Line south of Lucan.

"Barney had grown up in rural County Down," explained Peggy, "and his dream had always been to purchase a farm. We started looking around the London/Lucan area, but any farm we could afford we didn't like, and any that we liked we couldn't afford!"

That was until the caretaker at St. Patrick's school told Peggy of a farm for sale on the Roman Line. The Roman Line was named after the almost exclusively Roman Catholic settlers of the nineteenth century. The Rooneys were intrigued by the property located so close to the old Donnelly homestead. They had lived in Canada for thirteen years at this point and were well aware of the Donnelly saga. It became even more exciting when they learned that the home

for sale had once belonged to Patrick "Grouchy" Ryder. Ryder had been a neighbour of James and Johannah Donnelly for over thirty years. The two families were friends for the most part, until the day Grouchy's son James, a member of the Biddulph Vigilance Committee, participated in a search party of the Donnelly farm looking for a stolen cow. Johannah was furious and made a number of threats against young James Ryder. That was the end of their neighbourly friendship.

The Ryder farm, although rented out, had stayed in the family since the early 1800s. A grandson named Eddie Brown, who lived in nearby St. Marys, owned the property. Barney Rooney went to see Eddie Brown to discuss the possible sale of his farm. "It wasn't at all what I had expected," said Barney. "He was actually interviewing me for the job of buying his farm. It was quite perplexing. He wanted to know my name, where I'd come from, who my parents were, my complete life history. When he learned that I was a Catholic from Ireland, the deal was settled. I was thrilled, we shook hands, and that was it. I wondered in the name of God why I was getting the inquisition, which made no sense to me at the time. It wasn't until later that I found out that Brown was determined to carry on the Irish Roman Catholic tradition of his grandfather, who had purchased the farm from the Canada Company in the early 1840s."

The farmhouse had not been lived in for seventeen years, and flocks of birds and other species of wildlife had taken refuge in most of the structure. After taking possession of the farm in 1971, the Rooneys would spend every Saturday and Sunday not only cleaning up the house, but also enjoying the land and growing and tending vegetables, which was Peggy's passion. After acquiring two horses, they made the decision to permanently take on the rural lifestyle. The children, Hugh, Joyce, and two Canadian-born sons, Sean and Neil, had long beseeched their parents to move to the farm. They loved the freedom and the wide-open spaces to roam and could hardly wait for the big move into the country. Unfortunately that came upon the family quicker than expected. "Within a month we had to vacate our home. We had no choice but to move into the unfinished farmhouse. It took a tremendous effort on our part to make it liveable, but we did it," explained Peggy.

"And we didn't get divorced, either," Barney laughed.

"When we moved onto Grouchy Ryder's farm, we had read Orlo Miller's book *The Donnellys Must Die*, just to increase our knowledge about the Donnellys," said Peggy. "At that time, there was a real resurgence of interest in the Donnellys, and sightseers visiting St. Patrick's Church would drive past our house, down the Roman Line, searching for the Donnelly homestead. We were thrilled to own a piece of Canadian history."

After almost two decades of stewardship of Grouchy Ryder's farm, the Rooneys sold the property and moved back to London in 1998. When asked if they had carried on Eddie Brown's tradition of selling only to Irish Catholics, Barney and Peggy smiled and replied in unison: "Yes, we did!" The purchaser was their next-door neighbour, Phillip Harrigan, a Catholic and an Irish descendant.

Donnelly Authors

Orlo Miller

Orlo Miller died in 1993 at the age of eighty-two. The author-historian was considered to be one of the foremost experts on the Donnelly saga. He wrote *Death to the Donnellys*, a fictionalized account of the Donnelly story, and *The Donnellys Must Die*. In his book *The Donnellys Must Die*, published in 1962 by the Macmillan Company of Canada Ltd., Miller attempts to separate fact from fiction and legend from reality. It was his hope to convey to his readers the truth behind the Donnelly murders.

Orlo was born in London, Ontario, in 1911. He began his career in 1932 as a part-time correspondent for the *London Free Press*, joining the staff in 1940. He worked as a night telegraph editor, a science editor, and as a beat reporter. In 1944, he became a freelancer for CBC Radio. For the next quarter century, Orlo sold stories, documentaries, and plays not only to the CBC, but also to CBS in the United States and the BBC in England. Of the fifty plays he wrote, most of them were broadcast on radio. At the age of fifty-two, Orlo Miller changed his career path and became an Anglican priest. He served in Point Edward near Sarnia and in Mitchell, Ontario.

The following is a 1970 transcript of an interview between Miller and Frazer Boa, theatre critic for London's CFPL Television:

Boa: Orlo, eight years ago, your book was released and I remember sitting with you one night discussing the possibility of a film being made.

Miller: The book has been under option almost entirely since that time by different outfits.

Boa: What's the problem with it? Why hasn't it been made into a film before this?

Miller: The major problem has been the complicated nature of the story and the number of possible plot lines one could follow. Last year when I was in New York at 20th Century Fox, I discovered that every movie company in the United States had a copy of the book. They all saw its potential, but what has troubled them all is how to handle it.

Boa: Now there's an all-Canadian company that wants to do it. Where's it going to be shot? Is it going to be shot in Lucan?

Miller: (chuckle) No, I don't think so, Frazer, I don't think anyone would care to take the chance. It's not that we would anticipate any actual violence, although that always is a possibility. I think I can speak quite definitely for the people of Lucan and Biddulph that they wouldn't want it shot there! The community is too anxious to forget, and people like myself keep reminding them of what happened! What it is of course is a massive community guilt complex. After all, we must remember that more than 200 persons had guilty knowledge of this thing, either before or after the event, accessories before or after the crime. Many of these people have descendants still alive.

Boa: Where will the film be shot, Orlo?

Miller: It will be shot somewhere in this province. We may be using some of the many pioneer villages in Ontario. We may actually do some of the filming in the Lucan area.

Boa: Has the director or any of the cast been selected yet?

Miller: The director will be Bill Marshall of Marshall-Taylor, together with Glen-Warren Productions and John Bassett of the *Telegram*. This is a fully Canadian Company with Canadian money.

Boa: What will the budget be?

Miller: Something in the neighbourhood of a million dollars. Production is to begin this fall.

Was the movie ever made? As of this date, no one has taken up the challenge to produce a full feature movie of the Donnelly saga.

Ray Fazakas

In 1978, I received as a Christmas gift a book entitled *The Donnelly Album,* written by Ray Fazakas. Now dog-eared, it is my favourite chronicle of the Donnelly tragedy. *The Donnelly Album* and Ray's sequel, *In Search of the Donnellys*, share a special place on the bookshelf in my living room. Ray Fazakas is the pre-eminent Donnelly author. His work reflects extensive research and a great esteem for facts.

In 2003, I had the honour of meeting Ray in person at the Lucan Heritage Day Parade. We had both been invited to participate in the parade, riding in two separate convertible automobiles, very much enjoying being part of this special event. In February of the following year, I visited the retired lawyer-author at the home he shares with his wife Beverley near Hamilton, Ontario.

"My interest in the Donnelly story began in 1962 when I was thirty years old," said Ray. "I was listening to a CBC Radio review of Orlo Miller's new book, *The Donnellys Must Die*. I couldn't believe this tragic event had occurred a little over an hour's drive from my home. At that point I'd never heard of Thomas P. Kelley's book *The Black Donnellys*. I started thinking about the Donnelly massacre and just couldn't get it out of my mind. I started reading everything I could lay my hands on. I even packed my young family into the car and drove to Lucan's Roman Line, stopping in front of the old Donnelly schoolhouse for a picnic.

"The more I read, the more my curiosity peaked. Finally, I decided to do my own research, which eventually resulted in a book. It took me fifteen years to write that first book.

Donnelly author Ray Fazakas and Terry Culbert met for the first time in 2003. They both participated in the Annual Heritage Day Parade.

How do you find people in Lucan who will talk about that tragic time? I was an outsider and I didn't know anyone. I very quickly learned that you don't just go up to people on the street and ask them about the Donnellys! Mostly you are politely ignored, but at times you get a more direct response. I also learned that if you want the real Donnelly story, you don't ask the Protestants. They of course knew there were problems on the Roman Line and at St. Patrick's Parish, but they chose to mostly ignore it. From my legal perspective, I was amazed that after two trials no one was ever brought to justice. After the massacre occurred, the Catholic settlement closed up like a door that had been slammed shut. As long as the Vigilantes were alive, they could of course be charged with murder. In Canada, there is no statute of limitation on murder. The last of the alleged Vigilantes to die was John Joseph Lamphier in 1943. He died in Omaha, Nebraska.

"Did I ever have second thoughts writing about this unsolved crime? Actually, I had no hesitation writing about an event that took place over one hundred years ago. If this were a present-day event, of course, I'd use my discretion on how much to disclose. I was never out to slander anyone or cast a slight on people.

On the other hand, because of the passage of time, I didn't pull any punches, either. My premise is that if I'm really interested in a story, chances are that others are as well."

Ray graciously gave me a tour of his Donnelly room, where everything is catalogued. There are dozens upon dozens of small, wooden file drawers containing close to 200,000 records, which Ray is constantly updating.

Ray and his wife Beverley have been to Ireland twice. The first time was in 1978 after *The Donnelly Album* was published, and in 1988 they made their second trip. "We knew the area of North Tipperary where the Donnellys had come from," Ray said, "and we also knew that almost all of the Biddulph Irish originated from that area. A genealogist in Ireland did some research for me prior to our trip, which gave us a lot of background information."

Ray launched his second book, *In Search of the Donnellys,* at the Lucan Heritage Dinner in 2002. When asked if there would be another sequel, Ray looked at the audience and said: "It took me fifteen years to write my first book and twenty-five years to write my second. Just look at me, folks; there isn't going to be a third!" This is much to the disappointment of Ray Fazakas's faithful readers.

For copies of Ray Fazakas's books, contact:
B. Fazakas
942 King Street West
Hamilton, Ontario L8S 1K8

J. Robert Salts

I met J. Robert Salts at his home in 1990. As cameraman-producer for the Bramah, Ontario, segments shown on *Global Television News*, Bill Bramah and I were producing a segment on Salts, who lived with his family on the Donnelly homestead along the Roman Line. Bill and I were interested not only in the Donnelly story, but also in Salts, who was a practicing trans-clairvoyant at the time. The *Collin English Dictionary's* definition of a clairvoyant is "a person allegedly able to have the power of perceiving things beyond the natural range of the senses."

Living in a house rife with a turbulent history, Salts's supernatural perception seems an appropriate skill to have. The interview went well, and I did not speak with him for another thirteen years.

In March of 2003, I returned to visit J. Robert Salts to interview him for this book. I was interested to find out how he got involved in the Donnelly saga. He shared his Donnelly initiation with me, which truly happened serendipitously.

"I was attending London Teachers' College," said Robert. "I was with a group of student teachers joyriding the streets of London when Carol, one of the students, suggested we visit the Black Donnelly grave in Lucan. None of us had ever heard of the Black Donnellys. Eager for adventure, we drove to Lucan with Carol acting as a tour guide. She described the Donnelly massacre of February 4th, 1880, in great detail.

"As we pulled up to St. Patrick's Church at the corner of Highway 4 and the Roman line, it began to drizzle. Finding the gate locked, we

In May of 1881, William Donnelly had this house built on the site of his father James's first home. The photograph, taken around 1901, shows Robert Donnelly posing with his dog and nephew James, son of Michael.

Photograph courtesy of Ray Fazakas

The Salts family owns the house today. Additions to the front and back were constructed around 1971.

Photograph courtesy of author/homeowner J. Robert Salts

started climbing the four-foot-high chain-link fence. The wet, fallen leaves beneath our feet squished as we walked past the tall granite and marble tombstones. The markers were casting eerie shadows across the cemetery floor. We were all filled with anxious excitement.

"At one point, I noticed Carol standing on the spot where the coffins lay buried below her. I told her it might bring bad luck. To spite me, her brother Everett began stomping on the gravesite. In a hushed voice, for effect, I told him to stop and added that spitting on the soil will anger the spirits and they will surely come after all of us. Everett promptly spit and I let out a blood-curdling scream. Everyone bolted for the fence and with much difficulty tumbled over to the other side. After a tremendous amount of nervous laughter, and my assurance that I had not seen any angry spirit, the group forgave me. That was my exciting introduction to the Donnellys of Biddulph."

In his late thirties, Robert and his wife, Linda, decided to find a place in the country to live. Robert applied for a transfer and was accepted at the Biddulph Central School on Saintsbury Line in Lucan. The Saltses found a hobby farm not far from the new school. It was a property consisting of 6.19 acres, including a house, drive shed, and barn. "In 1988, Linda and I bought what turned out to be the old Donnelly homestead," Robert said with a grin on his face. "I was instantly flooded with memories of my first Donnelly encounter during my years attending teachers' college.

"It did not take long for the homestead to impel its effect on us. During our move, while unloading and carrying items into the barn, I had the unnerving sensation of being watched. With each trip, I felt the eeriness build. It was as if I were surrounded by unseen residents in that barn. Over the years, many visitors, some with developed psychic awareness, have experienced the same thing.

"Not only did we experience strange occurrences in the barn, but also in the house. Linda especially went through some nondescript depression whenever she worked in the kitchen. We decided to call the local Catholic priest to ask him to clear the house of unwanted spirits. Even though we are Protestants, we felt it important to involve a Catholic priest, based on the history of the home. The priest agreed to bless each and every room of our large house. Once the ritual was completed, we felt as though a burden was lifted from us and the kitchen no longer had any effect on Linda's mood.

"It seems, however, the priest did not exorcise all of the spirits from our homestead. During all times of the year I am often awakened in the middle of the night to the faint sounds of footsteps coming down the stairs from the bedrooms above. At first I thought it was our son Charles getting up for a drink, but every time I checked, he was sound asleep. No longer do I get up to check the stairs, only listen intently for each footfall and then go back to sleep. Not everyone in the house reacts that nonchalantly. Our dog, Jesse, a purebred German shepherd, absolutely refuses to go up the stairs to the second floor or go down to the basement."

After retiring as a teacher in 1995, Robert pursued his Donnelly Homestead Site Tours full time. A sign pounded into his front lawn invites people, for a small fee, to drop in or phone for an appointment. His tours have grown from ten minutes to a ninety-minute walkabout. During inclement weather, the tour takes place indoors, where he offers a "chair-side" chat next to a roaring fire. At times, Robert will brew up a large pot of tea for his visitors. When the weather permits, the tour begins at the north end of his house close to the site of the original Donnelly home. The tour always begins with Robert talking about the Donnellys' arrival in Upper Canada, explaining how they squatted on another person's land. The tour always ends with the story of a Donnelly relative selling the property in 1939 with a lot of interesting events in between.

"One gentleman, visiting with a group from Tipperary, Ireland, was so moved by what he heard that he cried several times during the story presentation. At the conclusion, he shook my hand and thanked me as more tears streamed down his face. I had no idea what he was saying because his thick Irish brogue was so thick. I wager it was not so much my storytelling that made him cry, but rather his own sensitivity to the topic," said Robert.

In 1996, J. Robert Salts self-published his book: *You Are Never Alone/ Our Life on the Donnelly Homestead*. That book has been revised and reprinted three times. If you're interested in visiting the Donnelly homestead, contact:

DONNELLY HOMESTEAD SITE TOURS
34937 Roman Line,
RR3 Lucan, Ontario N0M 2J0
(519) 227-1244

Other Donnelly Writers

Thomas P. Kelley

The Donnelly saga was introduced to me at the age of twelve by author Thomas P. Kelley in his book *The Black Donnellys: The True Story of Canada's Most Barbaric Feud*. Published by Harlequin Books of Winnipeg, Manitoba, in 1954, it sold for thirty-five cents, and I still have my copy. A few years later, he wrote a second book, *The Vengeance of the Black Donnellys*. According to many readers, Kelley was not a researcher of facts, but was the writer who put Lucan and the Donnellys on the map. Over half a century later, the subject of the Donnellys is more popular than ever.

James Reaney

Award-winning writer James Reaney's most famous work is his Donnelly Trilogy, three full plays about the Donnelly family of Biddulph Township. *Sticks and Stones*, the first play of his trilogy, was revived for Stratford's 2005 summer season. In 2004, The Champlain Society published *The Donnelly Documents: An Ontario Vendetta*, a collection of Donnelly documents, edited and introduced by Reaney. Nine hundred and twenty-five hardbound copies were printed; 875 went to Society members and subscribing libraries, and the remaining fifty copies were reserved for editorial purposes. Individual copies sold for one hundred dollars.

Peter Edwards

Night Justice: The True Story of the Black Donnellys was published by Key Porter Books in 2004. Called the first serious re-evaluation of Canada's most notorious crime, Peter Edwards's book draws on court transcripts, archival searches, and material obtained through the Freedom of Information Act.

Peter McKeown

The Donnelly Treatise: After the Massacre was self-published by Peter McKeown in 2004. It is a historical account of the Donnelly family survivors through the years 1880 to 1900. Visit **www3.simpatico.ca/pmckeown**

Donnelly Web Site

The Official Donnelly Home Page is a comprehensive Web site, full of information about the Donnellys. It is updated constantly with facts and photographs. **www.donnellys.com**

Actor Robert King, on the right, talks to Harry Hardy of the Lucan Area Heritage Society prior to his role as James Donnelly in playwright James Reaney's *Sticks and Stones*. The play was revived for Stratford's 2005 season.

HARDWARE

DE LAVAL CREAM SEPARATORS

PART THREE: *Poets, Historians and an Actor*

The Bard of Biddulph

William Wakefield Revington was born in Biddulph Township on the 9th of July 1843. He was the son of Irish immigrants Joseph Revington and Lydia Atkinson. His parents had left Ireland with two infant children, Joseph Jr. and his sister Ella. Ella died during the crossing and was buried at sea. After settling in Upper Canada, Joseph and Lydia reared seven more children, four girls and three boys, including William.

William, who grew up with the pioneer way of life, loved nature, loved his country, and most of all loved Biddulph Township. He was a farmer, a nurseryman, and a poet. In 1869 he married an Irish immigrant named Maria Carroll. Together they raised a family of nine children. Whenever time permitted, he used his poetry to express his love for land, people, and family.

Often under the pen name "Adare," his poems were published in many of the area newspapers. Nicknamed "The Bard of Biddulph," he was one of the most widely known writers of verse in Western Ontario. William's poetry was humorous, patriotic, and spoke of the people and events of his time. He wrote of births, deaths, and anniversaries. He created prose about the *Titanic* disaster and about the brave young men who fought in the Boer War and the First World War.

THE SAUBLE
by W.W. Revington (date unknown)

It was near the town of Lucan in the merry month of May,
Down by the river Sauble that I happened for to stray,
A river no as famous in the annals of our land,
As the "Shannon" was in Ireland, and they tell me that was grand.

At the bridge that spans the Sauble, north of London Road
Where poor old Jimmy Carrol had his little log abode:
What one time was a garden it is now in pasture lands,
And where stood his little cabin now the chimney only stands.

And yonder in the distance, down by the river shore,
Some gypsies are now camping where they often camped before:
Their campfire smoke ascending up to the azure blue,
And with the clouds all blending lends enchantment to the view.

Were I a landscape painter, it's here I'd try
my skill,
On the chrono of this valley and the famous
Sauble Hill:
But as I am not an artist now I hope I don't
intrude
If the picture I am painting may appear a
little rude.

For I love these hills and valleys, the river
and the glen.
If I can't paint their picture I can sketch
them with my pen.
In a way that's so peculiar you will wonder
when you see
If it interests your readers now the same as
it does me.

As a boy I often sported in its waters cool
and clear,
For our school was in the forest and the
river running near;
And many a time I rambled down by the
grassy shore
To see my darling Mary, now the one that I
adore.

And that little old log schoolhouse, it has
graduates today
In every town and city too, from here to
Baffin's Bay;
And the little Sauble rockers as we used to
call them then
Have outgrown their boyish capers and are
now our leading men.

Now readers do you wonder why the
Sauble won its fame,
For some of you were saying it's unworthy
of its name:
If there was no river Sauble let me tell you
as a friend
You would never know the comfort you had
camping at the Grand Bend.

CANADA
by W.W. Revington (January 19th, 1904)

Though "Bards" loved to sing of old Erin,
And called it the gem of the sea,
But find me a land that can equal
The land of our own maple tree.
A land that is loved and respected
Wherever her flag is unfurled,
That had freedom and land for its people,
And food to feed half the world.
It's here the oppressed of all nations,
Will find when they land on its shores,
It has farms to give for the asking,
And where is the land can give more.

To tell you of all its vast treasures,
'Tis more than I'm able to do,
But if it gives any pleasure,
I will try and mention you a few.
Her forests are counted the greatest,
Her gold mines are counted the best,
Her wheat and her cheese are the finest,
And her prairies the pride of the West.
It has silver and gold in its mountains,
And it has the finest soil,
It has clear, crystal water in fountains,
And beneath it abundance of oil.
It has all that the heart can desire,
Bestowed by a bountiful hand,
No wonder Canadians admire
And do love their own native lands.

On the 27th of July 1920, William
Wakefield Revington died at the home of his
daughter, Mrs. John Beaton. He was seventy-
seven years of age. William was buried in
Nursery Cemetery. He was survived by three
sons, four daughters, and twenty-eight
grandchildren.

The Poetic Policeman

HUGHIE CALLS THE DANCE
by Dave Egan

I've attended many socials in my life round
the earth,
I've seen the seamy side of life; I've had
my share of mirth,
I've drained the cup of bitterness; I've
tasted sweet romance,
But my greatest thrill was listening to Hugh
Toohey call a dance.
He was calling from the footlights of
Lucan's dancing hall,
And his noble, kingly stateliness impressed
us one and all;
I'm sure Caruso's singing to the haughty
dames of France,
Couldn't hold a light for Hughie, as he
called the Irish dance.
How the ladies sighed at seeing him, with
his gentle rhythmic motion,
A state of mind and body not induced by
any potion,
The singing seems to hold them in a
blissful, dreamy trance,
All the world is full of music, as he calls
the Irish dance.
They say they dance in Heaven and they
also dance below,

I won't grumble when they tell me which
place I have to go,
I'll consider myself lucky, if I only get a
chance,
To hear the sound of Hugh Toohey's voice,
as he calls the Irish dance.

Dave Egan, the author of the above poem,
was a romantic who wrote poetry all his life,
much to the delight of his wife, children,
relatives, and friends. He was inspired by the
style of American poet Edgar A. Guest. Dave's
poems were frequently published in the *Lucan
Sun*, a weekly newspaper. In July of 2003, I
spoke with the poet's eldest son, Dave, in his
east London home. Son Dave Jr., who was born
October 28th, 1918, in County Norfolk, England,
was eighty-five years old at the time of this
interview. His tremendous pride in, and
appreciation of, his father's talent was obvious
throughout our talk.

Dave Egan, his father, was born in 1888 in
County Cork, Ireland, the son of Bridget Mary
Power and David Thomas Egan. Young Dave
grew up with his brother, John, in the small
village of Kanturk near Cork City. In 1912, at
the age of fourteen, Dave and John decided to
see the world, and made their way across the
Atlantic to North America.

They arrived in New York City, staying with relatives in the Bronx, and soon found jobs working as streetcar conductors. After some time, Dave, the more adventurous of the two, convinced John to move to Detroit and then on to Windsor, Ontario. John, however, had become quite disillusioned and missed his homeland desperately. He returned to Ireland shortly thereafter.

Poetic policeman Dave Egan with his trusted terrier Paddy in the garden of his Market Street home.

Photo courtesy Winnie Egan

Dave had always been fascinated by the romantic depiction of hobos riding the rails. Left on his own, he was now able to follow his dream. He travelled by boxcar across the land until he reached Lake Louise, Alberta. It is not quite clear why or when he left Alberta, but he eventually returned to Windsor. Throughout all of his restless wandering, he kept notes and scribbled poems whenever he could.

This was the time of the First World War, and Dave was not to be left behind. He enlisted in the Canadian Army's 18th Battalion Infantry and was shipped to France. In 1916, a sniper's bullet ripped into Dave, ending his career as an active soldier. Dressed in his Canadian Army uniform, the young, wounded Irishman was transported from Courcelette, France, to a seaside hospital in Great Yarmouth, County Norfolk, England. While convalescing, one day he strolled past a knitting mill where he spotted a pretty young woman through the factory window. Dave waved and she waved back. Later he would recount: "I knew then, that's the girl I'm going to marry!" And he did. Ethel Kelf, the five-foot factory girl, and the five-foot eleven-inch soldier married after a short courtship. In 1918, Ethel gave birth to their first son, Dave Junior.

At the end of World War I, escaping grave economic times, Dave Sr. and his family returned to Canada, settling in London, Ontario. His first job was making cast-iron frying pans at the McClary plant. Before long he moved on to something that was near and dear to his heart. He worked as a psychiatric orderly at Westminster Hospital, dealing with shell-shocked veterans.

Dave and Ethel's second son, Francis Henry, was born on the 9th of November 1919. With two young children and a wife to support, Dave took a position with the Ford Motor Company in Windsor. His wages amounted to $7.00 per day, a substantial sum at that time. In 1939, Dave moved to Lucan, making his home on Market Street. He embarked on a new career, becoming Lucan's police constable.

When the Second World War broke out in Europe, both Dave's sons enlisted in the Royal Canadian Army. Dave Jr. joined the Elgin Regiment in June of 1940. Frank joined the Corps of Engineers.

"During the war years, Dad became a big hit with the local boys in Lucan," Dave Jr. recalls. "He started an amateur boxing club. The workouts were held in the fire station, the only large hall available. The fire truck was moved outside to make room for the eager boys. Adults who stopped by to watch usually dropped a few coins into Dad's police hat. Those donations went toward the purchase of gloves and equipment for the young boxers.

"Both my parents were involved in the community and well known for their good deeds. My mother sewed dozens of boxing trunks for the team to wear. Dad understood that the young boys needed a place to go, to build confidence, character, and strong muscles. Dad got a lot of support from a broad-minded reeve and council."

A visitor to Lucan from New York observing the boxing team was quoted in the *London Free Press*:

This little village of Lucan is a great example to more prosperous towns and cities. Whilst everybody is talking of the morals of youth, Lucan seems to be doing something about it. A little village that has the heart to tackle a job of that kind [the boxing club] at a time like this deserves the highest award that can be conferred on it. They are building something in a world where everything is torn down.

"My father was not only the village policeman, but also the dogcatcher, truant officer, and the garbage inspector," Dave Jr. said. "He was never afraid to speak up. I remember when Dad approached Council asking for a pay increase; he was told to do more policing. When he asked what else he could possibly do, it was suggested that, for example, he issue a parking ticket to the car illegally parked across the street. Dad correctly pointed out that the council member himself repeatedly parked in that exact spot. Well, Dad got his raise without ever writing any parking tickets. I can't help wondering, though, how effective Dad was as a constable, making only one arrest in all his years of policing Lucan."

His one and only arrest was written up in the *London Free Press*:

Appearance of John Hannon, 53, no permanent address, in County Court today, spoiled the three-year no-arrest record of Chief Dave Egan in the peaceful Village of Lucan. Hannon was charged with assaulting 74-year-old Henry Henson, military medal winner in the First World War, and occasioning actual bodily harm. The case was adjourned until Tuesday, after Crown Attorney Claude Savage said Henson was injured to such an extent that he was unable to appear in court. Chief Egan, making his first arrest in three years, picked up Hannon at the home of John Clark, Lucan. Clark was charged with permitting drunkenness in his home and the case was enlarged [sic] until Tuesday.

September 25th, 1944, was a tragic day for the Egan family. Their son Frank was killed in action overseas while fighting with the 8th Reconnaissance of 14th Hussars. He is buried at Bergen op Zoom in Holland. He left behind his young wife, Kit, and infant sons Frank and Pat. Besides his family, Dave Egan had another big love in his life: his little terrier, the runt of the litter, which he named Paddy. Walking Paddy on his evening rounds inspired this poem:

CHILLY, FLASH and BILLY
by Dave Egan

When the evening's growing chilly
I get out my flash and Billy
And go strolling with auld Paddy by me side,
He's as happy as can be, chasing squirrels up a tree
To the cat that gets cornered, woe betide.
When we run into a blizzard that would freeze your very gizzard
And I can plainly hear his chattering teeth.
When the bitter wind is blowin' and its

home he should be goin'
He just curls up and sleeps between me feet.
When the spaleen starts a fightin'
And Bud Stanley's dog is biting
And Paddy looks like losing his valise,
Maybe then I'll take the notion
For to start the law in motion
And I'll bind Bud's little dog to keep the peace.
When he starts to pull his capers
Chasin' tractors, then be japers
I can feel me scanty hair stand on me head.
I'm afraid that William Haskett
Will have Paddy in a basket,
And the beat will be so lonely when he's dead.
If Paddy gets knocked over by Ben Morrisey, the Drover,
Sure there's one thing will console me for the loss.
On a pair of me auld brogans, he'll be resting with the Dogans
Waiting patiently in heaven for his boss.

As a young child growing up in Lucan, my parents' home was directly across the street from Dave and Ethel Egan's. I can still picture Mr. Egan's friendly face, his lilting Irish accent, and the police uniform he smartly wore with pride.

Much of this story was relayed to me by the poetic policeman's son Dave Jr., sitting at his kitchen table. Sadly he passed away in his eighty-sixth year on June 15th, 2004. David Jr. is survived by his wonderful wife, Winnie (Winnifred Erma White), ten children, thirty-one grandchildren, twenty-seven great-grandchildren and one great-great-grandchild.

Lucan Actor Plays Dublin

On the eleventh of July 2003, my first cousin Jeff Culbert and I sipped Guinness in an Irish pub on Talbot Street in London, Ontario. Owned by Dubliner Pat Keogan, The Last Drop had the perfect ambience to record an interview with Jeff about his one-man show he took to Ireland. My cousin is an actor and the artistic director and founder of Ausable Theatre.

Although it originated in Lucan, Ausable Theatre now makes its home in London, most often performing at the Grand's McManus Studio Theatre.

"Having grown up in Lucan of Irish descendants," said Jeff, "I've always had an interest in Ireland and have visited the country twice. On my first trip, I had the pleasure to attend the Dublin Theatre Festival and the Dublin Fringe Festival. I remember walking around the city thinking, *Okay, I*

WORK

BY JAMES O'REILLY
FEATURING JEFF CULBERT

"HOWLINGLY FUNNY. . .JARRINGLY SURREAL" TORONTO GLOBE AND MAIL

Andrews Lane Theatre, St Andrews Lane, Dublin 2
Sept 23 - Oct 5 (except Sunday), 6pm
€6 - €8, 1850 374 643
Ausable Theatre, London, Ontario, Canada

do theatre, why don't I bring a show here next year?

"It took me three years of agonizing over various plays, trying to incorporate all that was involved to take one overseas. I decided to do a one-man show. All I would need is a stage manager. I applied to the Dublin Fringe Festival and to my great excitement I was accepted. The name of the show was *WORK*, by Canadian playwright James O'Reilly. He grew up in Toronto, in a rough, low-rent neighbourhood. O'Reilly was thrilled to learn that I was taking his show to Ireland."

In the fall of 2002, Jeff brought O'Reilly's play to the land of their ancestors. In the heart of Dublin City, not far from Trinity College and the River Liffey, Jeff performed *WORK* in the Andrews Lane Studio on St. Andrews Lane. "The seventy-seat theatre was a black box of a room," said Jeff. "Some of the seats were torn and ragged, but it gave the small theatre character."

Jeff Culbert performed *WORK* on stage at the Andrews Lane Studio in Dublin, Ireland.

Jeff with his older brother Peter and younger brother Tim, an actor working and living with his family in Alberta. Behind are the boys' cousins, Dana Garrett and her brother, the author.

Jeff received glowing reviews from Ireland's major newspapers, including *The Irish Examiner*:

One thing which death can't kill off is the enduring popularity of the monologue. Strictly speaking though, *WORK* is less of a monologue and more of a one-man show as Canadian actor and artistic director of Ausable Theatre Jeff Culbert brings us through a variety of blue-collar losers in James O'Reilly's play.

With great humour and a script slick as paraffin, Culbert gives us the waiter who snorts cocaine and reveals the *mesprise* [scorn] and street suss that enables him to survive in his job and sort out the tippers from the meanies of his customers. There's a nice vignette of the sorts of places we eat in and how they reflect our new dichotomy between alternative and straight ways of living. There's Jim the meat packer who turns Jim the garbage man, and Jim the sewer worker who turns high-flying, adrenaline-fuelled whiz kid copy ad writer.

The juxtapositions of each of the transformations are full of purpose and wittily restore a revealing and not flattering link. Culbert is mesmerizing, an ensemble rolled into one.

"The arts are a way of life in Ireland," explains Jeff. "There's all that literature, music, and theatre. It is such an inspirational place. The Irish have always been an inspired people, regardless of the ups and downs of their lives. They are very prolific. They love to talk and they love to tell stories around the kitchen table and in their pubs. That love of the gab spills onto the stage. All this brilliance of conversation, ear for music, and talent in one place.

"The Abbey Theatre in Dublin is one of the greatest theatre institutions in the world. The number of Irish plays at any given time is huge, as are the numbers of new writers. Many of the plays are premieres and reflect current society and culture. This isn't just the past they're bringing out. Ireland is more prosperous than it has ever been, certainly in modern history, and the theatre is reflecting that. I always have an eye on the Irish playwrights because I feel they're excellent."

So how did Jeff get into theatre full time? Jeff's mom, my Aunt Muriel, was instrumental in changing his life's vocation. She'd found an audition notice for an upcoming production of *Jesus Christ Superstar*. She knew how much Jeff and his brothers Mike, Peter, and Tim had loved that show and were constantly singing all of the show tunes. Jeff accepted his mother's suggestion, auditioning and landing the role of

Judas Iscariot at the University of Western Ontario's Talbot College Theatre.

"I'd always loved theatre, but never taken it seriously," said Jeff. "I'd do a show, perhaps every three years. When *Jesus Christ Superstar* ended, I thought, well there's my theatre for the next three years. That was not to be, as I was asked to do another play, and then another. I was approached to direct a show, which was a whole new experience for me. I loved the challenge and enjoyed it immensely. With all this experience under my belt, I decided to strike out on my own, and in 1998, I started The Ausable Theatre Company."

Jeff has brought many successes to his theatre company over the years. During the summer of 2005, he directed a new play by Chris Doty called *The Donnelly Trial*. It is based on the two trials of the accused Vigilantes who allegedly murdered five members of the Donnelly family on the 4th of February 1880. Jeff is one of those rare people, living his dream, doing what he loves and what he does best.

Historian A.S. Garrett

I don't remember ever meeting Scott Garrett. I knew almost everyone in our village of 900, but had never made Scott's acquaintance, even though his nephew Jack Garrett married my sister Dana.

Alfred Scott Garrett was born in 1906 on the London Township farm that had been in his family since 1850, purchased by his great-grandparents, who had emigrated from Ireland. In 1938, Scott's parents, Alfred and Amanda Garrett, sold the farm and moved into the village of Lucan. A bachelor all of his life, Scott came with them. He worked full time for the Hay Stationery Company in London. Much of his spare time was devoted to his love for history and music. He played banjo in a band called The Melody Boys Orchestra with fellow musicians Lorne Grose and Adam Brock. They were a popular dance band during the 1930s.

Scott's first love, however, was local history. He spent a lifetime researching, writing articles, and taking photographs of local places and their inhabitants. Many long hours were spent in area cemeteries collecting and cataloguing what proved to be valuable and accurate information. Under the byline A.S. Garrett, his historical research was frequently published in the "Looking Over Western Ontario" section of *The London Free Press*.

Scott Garrett died in 1964 at the age of fifty-eight. Scott's brother William donated all his archival material, photographs, and negatives to the J.J. Talman Regional Collection at the University of Western Ontario in London. A couple of the photographs in this book were taken by Scott Garrett. It is because of people like Scott that an abundance of local history is being shared by, and passed on to, future generations.

Photo courtesy University of Western Ontario Archives

Alfred Scott Garrett

Brothers of History

The Hodgins name has been linked with Biddulph Township since Adam Hodgins emigrated from Ireland in 1831. Probably the most famous Hodgins to emigrate was James "Big Jim" Hodgins of Borrisokane, Tipperary, also arriving that same year. James became a land agent for the Canada Company, helping to relocate many of his fellow Irishmen to the area. He became the first clerk of Biddulph and was elected the first reeve. He was justice of the peace and a whisky distiller. Hodgins was a very good friend of James Donnelly Sr. and on one of Hodgins's trips back to Ireland, he brought James's wife Johannah and their son James Jr. to Upper Canada, thus reuniting the family.

Within ten years of James Hodgins's arrival, close to four dozen different Hodgins households were established in Biddulph Township, all of them Irish Protestants, and all from North Tipperary.

Very few Biddulph township councils have been elected without at least one Hodgins as either reeve or councillor. It all began in 1850, when Colonel James "Big Jim" Hodgins was elected the first reeve of Biddulph. Starting with James, the following are his descendants who have served their community as reeve of Biddulph:

1850–51	Col. James "Big Jim" Hodgins (the founder of Biddulph)
1855–56	John Hodgins (son of "Big Jim")
1856–58	Thomas Hodgins
1858–64	H.B. Hodgins
1872–77	John Hodgins
1887–97	Charles Constantino Hodgins (grandson of "Big Jim")
1897–1901	A.K. Hodgins
1901–02	S.H. Hodgins
1909–14	A.K. Hodgins
1922–23	R.E. Hodgins
1955–61	Austin Hodgins
1964–77	Wilson Hodgins
1979–89	Wilson Hodgins

Today, Hodgins is still one of the most common names in the area. Hamilton Hodgins and his late younger brother Austin held a deep appreciation for history, especially the history of their family and township. If not for these two men, much of the local area history would have been lost. Prior to Austin's death at the age of eighty-two, he coordinated and partially wrote a 682-page book entitled *Pioneers to the Present, Biddulph Township 1850–2000*. With the invaluable assistance of Township Deputy Clerk-Treasurer Joan Goddard and a book committee of two dozen volunteers, Austin oversaw the hardbound, picture-filled compilation to its published form.

According to his daughter Jackie Martens, Austin was always writing. "He wrote about his horses, his thoughts of being overseas during the Second World War, and any other event in his life. Dad was a wonderful storyteller, but never expressed the desire to write a book. I even bought him a small tape recorder, but he refused to use it.

"He was a true Canadian in every sense of the word. Even when it came time to pay his income tax, he always said that the government needs the money to run this wonderful country. His love for Biddulph Township went so far that he disliked travelling outside of the area. According to him, this was the greatest place in the world."

Hamilton Hodgins certainly shared his brother's love for the land and for Biddulph Township. "I had promised my wife, Audrey, that I would retire by the time I reached the age of sixty-five," he said, "but when the time came, I was far from ready to quit farming. Audrey agreed to carry on a bit longer, and we stayed one more year. After selling off the livestock, we moved from Whalens Corners to Lucan." Hamilton now lives in a comfortable, well-maintained bungalow on George Street with his wife and their son Burton. "It was a sudden change to go from doing chores every day to suddenly doing nothing. As I had no real hobbies, I decided to write my memoirs to leave a legacy for my children and grandchildren."

Hamilton spent two winters writing his first booklet, *Reflections*. It is his account of growing up on the Coursey Line. In addition, he wrote about Lucan during the 1920s, the railroad, Scotts Elevator, and Langford Lumber. *Tales of Long Ago* is based on dozens of interviews with seniors at the Lucan's Sunshine Club. In 1996, Hamilton finalized *Whalen Corners Review*, life on his farm with Audrey and their children. Hamilton's writings have never been published. His typewritten manuscripts are photocopied for relatives and friends.

Brothers Hamilton and Austin were born on the family farm situated on the Coursey Line. Hamilton was born on September 13th, 1918, the eldest child of Mary Jane Lucinda (Lulu) Reith and J. Oscar Hodgins. Austin was born in 1920, followed by Gwendolyn, Vincent, Genevieve, and Lawrence.

"There was always a lot of life and laughter in our large family," remembered Hamilton. "When I was thirteen and Austin eleven, my Uncle Arnold decided to teach all the children how to dance. Accompanied by my father on fiddle and Mother on piano, Uncle Arnold called the dance. Aunt Estelle showed the boys how to fox trot, waltz, and two-step, while Uncle Arnold taught the girls."

Those dancing skills have served the brothers well. "In 1941, the Ontario Department of Agriculture held a course in Lucan, teaching the boys new ways of farming and the girls home economics," recalls Hamilton. "At the end of a gruelling day, a dance was held at the Stanley Opera House. My sister Gwen introduced me to a black-haired beauty with a twinkle in her eye. We danced all night, and a year and a half later I married Audrey Grose."

Brother Austin also met his future wife at a dance. At the time, he was a soldier stationed in

Holland waiting to be shipped home. "Austin was a very shy young man, and it took a lot of cajoling from his army buddies before he asked a pretty young woman to dance," recalls Austin's daughter Jackie Martens. "He must have impressed her with his dancing skill."

Even though it took six years and a lot of correspondence across the Atlantic, Dolly finally travelled to Canada to marry Austin. Both brothers carried on the family tradition of farming and both had two children. "My father loved his farm, loved his family, and loved history. History was definitely his great passion," said Jackie.

Hamilton is very proud of the tremendous amount of work and dedication his brother gave to the Biddulph Township book and the research he put into their family tree. He notes: "As far back as I can remember, both Austin and I had a great interest in history. During my high school years, I didn't give a darn about the War of the Roses or ancient history. Canadian history, on the other hand, had my undivided attention. I loved it then and I love it now!"

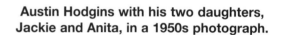

Austin Hodgins with his two daughters, Jackie and Anita, in a 1950s photograph.

Hamilton Hodgins and retired veterinarian Doctor Lloyd Hall on the left, at a 2004 steam threshing demonstration near Lucan.

PART FOUR: *Village Commerce*

.STANLEY
ARDWARE

McCLARY'S
SUNSHINE FURNACE
&
PANDORA RANGE

Circa 1900 photograph courtesy Stanley family

Village Funeral Parlours

In the 1950s, in our pre-teens, my friends and I spent countless hours guessing the make of new automobiles as they passed through Lucan. Was it a Pontiac or a Chevrolet? Those two looked identical except for the nameplate. Strolling home from public school one warm spring day, we were doing just that. By the time we reached Mike Murdy's house, we had tired of our game and eagerly accepted his invitation to see the new coffins his father had on display above their funeral parlour. Most of us had been inside a funeral home before, but this was going to be something very different. As Mike opened the door at the top of the stair, a view to behold greeted us. We saw a room full of highly polished caskets of different makes adorned with fancy handles. They looked enormous to us. We considered that if the caskets had had four rubber tires, this could be a showroom for new automobiles, and we would be playing a different guessing game.

Mike's father was the third generation to operate the Murdy Funeral Home. It was Mike's great-grandfather John Murdy who founded it in 1872. It was also his great-grandfather who prepared the deceased Donnellys for their burial after the massacre. That included sixty-three-year-old James Donnelly Sr., his fifty-six-year-old wife, Johannah, son John, thirty-two, and son Tom, twenty-five. James's niece, twenty-one-year-old Bridget, visiting from Ireland, was also murdered that night. John Murdy placed the body of John Donnelly in one coffin and the charred remains of the other four in a second casket. On the 6th of February, a procession stretching almost half a mile in length made its way from Lucan to St. Patrick's Church on the Roman Line for the funeral of the Donnellys. It included at least 500 mourners and dozens of teams of horses and sleighs. It truly was a sight to be seen.

John Murdy continued to run his funeral home until his death in April 1915, at which time his son Clifton James took over. Known as Cliff, he is remembered as a star baseball player with the Lucan Irish. Cliff's son John (Jack) Clifton Murdy was licensed in 1933. He, too, was involved in sports, coaching the Lucan Girls' Softball Team. Jack's son Mike became the fourth generation to carry on the tradition. He apprenticed at the George E. Logan and Son Funeral Home in London, where his father had taken his apprenticeship years before. After receiving his licence, Mike decided to stay in London rather than return to Lucan. He joined the A. Millard George Funeral Home in London and has been a funeral director with them for over four decades.

Mike's father, Jack, died in 1975. His would become the last funeral to be held in the

John's son Cliff

His grandson Jack

His great-grandson Mike

John Murdy stands at the door to his funeral parlour. It was John that buried the Donnelly family.

Murdy Funeral Home. Jack's burial was officiated by his long-time friends from Stephenson Funeral Home in Ailsa Craig. After Jack's death, Murdy Funeral Home closed its doors 103 years after first opening in 1872.

When asked if he can remember any unusual experiences during his lengthy career, Mike Murdy recalled the following: "It was a rain-soaked day in March as I assisted two elderly women to the graveside of a friend. Manoeuvring between the tombstones in the slushy, snow-covered graveyard, the earth below my feet suddenly gave way. I disappeared into wet snow up to my waist. As the temperature had risen, the ground had heaved and imploded with the impact of my weight. I was now literally three feet down; stuck in a hole. After making sure I was okay, my two elderly companions barely gave me another glance, and quickly walked away in their eagerness not to miss the funeral service."

Will there be a fifth generation of Murdys in the funeral business? Although Mike's sons Chris and Jeff have both put themselves through school working part-time at the A. Millar George Funeral Home, they have no desire to make it a career.

Down the street from Murdy's, Lucan boasted a second funeral parlour called the C. Haskett and Son Funeral Home. One Saturday morning when I was home from high school, I received a telephone call from my father's friend Clarence Haskett, the funeral director. He had a strange request. Clarence required photographs of a deceased woman who was resting in her coffin. Clarence knew I was a decent photographer and, although only sixteen, I was shooting news photographs for the *London Free Press* and the *Exeter Times Advocate* when not in school.

I was more than a little apprehensive about this assignment, although once I'd arrived and spoken with Clarence, my concerns dissipated. "She has very few relatives or friends living in this area," Clarence explained. "In order to make this part of their beloved's event, I need you to take a variety of pictures to be distributed to her absentee family." I composed a wide shot of the room showing the casket at one end adorned with containers of flowers. Then Clarence handed me a small stepladder. "I also require an overhead, Terry, looking straight down on the old darling," he said. My apprehension returned as I focused my twin lens reflex on the dead woman's face. I've often thought of those black and white images. Did the pictures help the family in their time of grief, or did the photographs cause more pain?

It was Clarence's grandfather Charles who established the business in 1882, ten years after John Murdy founded his funeral home. Charles purchased an existing business at the corner of Main and Market Streets from cabinetmaker/undertaker Albert Goodacre. In those days, the cabinetmaker was also the one called on to make the caskets. At that time, the body of the deceased for the most part wasn't displayed at the funeral home. The embalming process, visitation, and funeral service all took place in the home of the dead person's family.

Charles Haskett remained active until his death in 1945, at which time he was believed to be the oldest funeral director in the province of Ontario. Charles's son William, who had joined

Bill Haskett, great-grandson of Charles, the founder, is the fourth generation to operate the Lucan Funeral Service.

C. HASKETT, UNDERTAKER

Photos courtesy of Bill Haskett

his father in 1918, ran the business until his death in 1961. William's youngest son Clarence became the third generation of the Haskett family in the funeral business.

When the Hasketts ceased to make cabinets of their own, they sold ready-made furniture. As that business grew, more space was needed for display purposes. In 1962, Clarence negotiated the purchase of the present funeral home property on Main Street. The handsome yellow brick mansion was known as the old Stanley Estate or Stanley Hall. Barney Stanley built the showplace in the mid-1800s. Clarence Haskett, his wife, Eileen, and their three children moved to spacious living quarters above the new funeral home. Bill, the eldest of the siblings, was licensed in 1971 and worked alongside his father until Clarence decided to officially retire on the first of January 1998.

In 1990, Bill expanded the family business, purchasing the Hooper Hockey Funeral Home in Exeter. Two years later, they closed their furniture store, and the original building was sold. Bill and Clarence donated many artefacts and original "undertaker" equipment to Fanshawe Pioneer Village in London.

C. Haskett and Son and Hooper Hockey Funeral Services are two of the most progressive funeral homes in southwestern Ontario. They offer personalized colour photo cards and on-line condolences on their Web site. Bill also offers tours, speaks to various groups, and organizes grief seminars.

Bill and his wife, Sue, have three children. Erin is a Vancouver film producer and Jennifer is a nutritionist in Halifax. Only Colin, the youngest, obtained his licence; thus, the fifth generation of Hasketts is firmly ensconced in the funeral business.

Lankin Family Gas Station Since 1928

The Lankin family has been part of Lucan's business community since Harry E. Lankin opened his harness-making shop in 1910. Along with his helper, Don Chown, he produced complete sets of new harnesses and repaired old, worn ones. Harry, an astute entrepreneur, could see the writing on the wall and foresaw a new era in transportation dawning in the 1920s. Already a handful of Lucanites had purchased the new-fangled invention called the automobile.

Harry bought the present family location on the corner of Main and Water Streets and in 1927 he opened Lucan's first gas station, pumping White Star gasoline. However, Harry did not cast aside the horse population, but continued to make and repair harnesses. The model horse used by Harry and Don to measure and fit harnesses eventually found a new home in the Lucan Museum.

In 1928, Harry formed an alliance with the Shell Oil Company of Canada, and a two-bay service garage was added. By 1934, Jack Lankin had joined his father's business, adding a grocery department and a full-sized apartment above the store. The early gasoline dispensers were tall and elegant, sporting a glass cylinder containing fuel. Each time a vehicle was filled with gas, the attendant refilled the glass cylinder with a hand-pump.

With the onset of the Second World War, Jack enlisted in the Canadian Army and was sent overseas. His father, his sister Jean, and his wife, the former Kay Revington, ran the operation in his absence. Upon his return, Jack resumed running the business with the help of his dad.

After Jack's father, Harry, died in 1962, Jack and his son Don took over the business. Over the years, the Lankin Shell Station expanded to include a variety of customer services. They not only pumped gas, but also became a fully stocked convenience store, a recycling depot for beer bottles, and a pet food depot. They sell and repair tires and carry out minor automotive work. While buying your lottery tickets, you can have your ice skates sharpened. How is that for outstanding customer service?

In 1962, Don married Dorothy Lynn. They had a daughter, Carolynn, and a son, Paul. As soon as the children were old enough, they, too, worked in the business. Carolynn continued working part time, and Paul joined the operation full-time after completing high school. The Lankin gas station is now a fourth-generation family-owned enterprise.

The Lankins were honoured in 1989 for being the longest family-owned and -operated Shell gas station in Canada. The award presentation and dinner was held at L'Hotel in Toronto. Jack MacLeod, president of Shell Canada, made the presentation to the Lankins on their sixtieth anniversary.

In 1996, *Shell Marketing*, an in-house magazine, published an article on the Lankins, praising their sixty-eight years in the business.

They quoted Don Lankin as saying: "I've seen gasoline prices rise from thirty-nine cents a gallon to sixty cents a litre—or about $2.70 a gallon—since I started."

Today, the gas pumps are fully computerized, and long gone are those great-looking, tall, hand-pumped dispensers. When I return to Lucan for a visit, the old gas station still looks great. Fortunately, Shell Canada has had the wisdom not to rip down the old and

Harry E. Lankin, Harness Maker

replace it with a new self-serve gas bar. For the local drivers and those motoring through, four generations of the Lankin family have built up an impressive level of customer loyalty. "The real key to long-term survival in this business is treating your customers right and being part of the community," Don said. "We've always believed in going the extra mile to please our patrons."

"Our business is constantly changing," said Paul Lankin, "and we have to be ready to change with it!" Paul and his wife, Melanie, have two young sons, Eric and Matthew, and a daughter named Grace. Will the Lankin name continue for a fifth generation? Only time will tell.

In 1927, Harry opened Lucan's first gas station.

Lucan Cold Storage

As a child of the forties, I remember preserving food in an icebox. Years later, my parents purchased a refrigerator with a tiny freezing compartment just large enough to hold one ice-cube tray. It certainly wouldn't hold a quarter of beef and the various preserves my mother put down each fall. Recognizing a need, Harold Corbett provided a unique service for anyone needing to freeze larger food items. He opened the Lucan Cold Storage.

I loved it when Mom sent me to pick up a frozen roast for Sunday dinner during the hottest days of summer. I remember stepping through the front door, greeting Mr. Corbett as he carved steaks, chops, and roasts for one of his customers. He'd wrap the meat in brown waxed paper, writing the contents and date on the package with a thick black crayon.

Pulling open a heavy insulated door, I'd step into a second room. The temperature was considerably cooler, preserving the carcasses of beef and pork hanging from the ceiling on long hooks. For anyone the least squeamish, this easily might have been the catalyst to becoming a vegetarian. Opening a door to the third room, I encountered even colder temperatures. With key at the ready and my breath producing clouds of vapour, I opened the padlock to my parents' rented locker. It was not prudent to remain any longer than necessary as goose bumps by then covered my entire body. Taking out what Mom had requested, I locked the padlock. Racing back towards the street, the two heavy doors clanging shut behind, I was once more in the sweltering heat of summer.

Robert Hill O'Neil originally constructed the cold storage building as a private bank. The bank opened on the 27th day of September 1876. After O'Neil died in 1901, his son Aljoe sold it to the Merchants' Bank. They eventually moved across the road to the corner of Main and Alice streets. Today the building has been transformed once again. Instead of cold hands and goose bumps, I can now warm my hands with a bowl of steaming hot soup or a cup of coffee.

The Little Store with the Big Stock

After serving with the Royal Canadian Air Force during World War II, my father decided to return to the area of his childhood. It was 1947, and Dad was working as a regional salesman for Irwin Toys of Toronto. Forever enterprising, it wasn't long before he made up his mind to go into business for himself. With my mother's blessing, he opened a store. The first location was in a leased building at the north end of the business block. Although the dwelling has since been torn down, it stood very close to the present-day post office. To make ends meet, my twenty-seven-year-old father farmed at night for the first year, growing soybeans. He rented 100 acres on the Coursey Line, a stone's throw from the farm where he and his five brothers grew up.

Working in the store during the day and farming at night was gruelling. To make matters worse, business at that end of the block was anything but brisk. When the opportunity arose to purchase a store in the heart of the business section, Dad and Mom acted quickly. They bought their new building, sold our home on Market Street, and moved us into the apartment above the store. Over the years, the business went by two different names: Mel Culbert's Five Cents to a Dollar Store and Mel Culbert Dry Goods and Variety Store. Dad's slogan for the latter was: "The Little Store with the Big Stock."

As my parents increased their holdings, they purchased the building next door. With clothing sections for men, women, and children, it resembled a small-town department store. Our pride was a family of mannequins that displayed the clothes, standing in the storefront windows. Dad sold yard goods, linoleum, candy, and cosmetics, among other things. Christmas was an especially exciting time, as the toy department expanded. Dad let me assemble a make-believe village called Plasticville. The main attraction was a smoking electric train, which chugged and shunted its way through the little toy village. I spent hours assembling the little village and operating the train.

In order to move his merchandise, my father held a large sale a few times each year. His mode of advertising was distribution of printed flyers. I loved accompanying Dad to the printing shop located on the outskirts of nearby Centralia. With eyes wide open, I watched the craftsman as he set the type, one lead letter at a time. It was exciting to see the first impressions on paper made by the type, which was coated in black ink. When the run was over, Dad and I brought the stacks of freshly printed flyers home. Sitting at the kitchen table, my sister Dana and I folded the advertisements for delivery. The next day, I proudly pedalled my balloon-tire bike with its newspaper basket filled

Mom, Dad, and sister Dana in front of our Market Street home just prior to moving to the apartment above the store.

Dana and Terry ride a stagecoach through the author's bedroom in 1956.

to the brim with flyers. Making my way to each and every door, I made sure all households in Lucan received our sale information. It felt very important to be part of the family business.

Oney McFalls and Evelyn Young worked in the store as two very competent saleswomen. They lived in the village with their respective families. Each afternoon, my dad would send Oney and Evelyn upstairs to have tea and homemade baked goods with my mother, Mary. Dad always appreciated his employees and did not take them for granted. He had an easygoing manner with staff and customers alike.

He loved showing special attention to his female customers, and harmless flirting and teasing was very much part of his nature. I especially remember June Weller, mother of my best friend, Tom. She was a robust, good-natured woman, who was a regular shopper at our store. Each time she walked through the door, Dad would break into song: "June is busting out all over!" She blushed and giggled, loving the attention showered on her. Mrs. Weller was also known as an excellent baker, and quite often brought Dad a loaf of her homemade bread, still warm from the oven, which was enjoyed by all of us.

Sister Dana and I had bedrooms at the rear of our apartment. From the second-floor windows, we overlooked the Central Hotel parking lot. At night, after our parents had tucked us safely into our beds, Dana and I, with our noses pressed against the cool windowpane, watched the nightly activities behind the hotel. With a mixture of fear and thrill, we observed tipsy patrons making their way home, quite often taking a swing at each other. Shades of the Donnelly era, perhaps.

Our evening entertainment changed when we acquired a television set. We were the second home in Lucan to do so. Television pictures in the early fifties were black and white. I remember the day Dad came into the living room carrying a small sheet of plastic and promptly taped its corners to the screen. Our curiosity piqued, we asked what it was. "It's going to give us colour television," he said. The high-tech invention gave the illusion of colour: shades of blue for sky, pink for flesh tones, and green for grass. Our home became the envy of all our friends.

I fondly remember wintry Saturday nights in our cosy apartment. My dad's friend Bob Murray often came over to watch *Hockey Night in Canada* with us. We all sat around the television set cheering on the Toronto Maple Leafs. At the end of the game, Mom brought in steaming hot cups of tea and cinnamon toast for everyone. We'd settle in to watch Bob and Dad's favourite CBC female singer, *Our Pet Julliette*. Even though I was only thirteen years old at the time, I certainly understood the appeal of Julliette, which wasn't necessarily her voice. Julliette was well endowed and eventually capitalized on this with her own bra line. If I remember correctly, Dad carried "Our Pet Julliette" brassieres in his store. He was her keen supporter.

It was an enormous loss for all of us when Dad died in 1958 at the young age of thirty-eight.

Duke, the Milkman's Horse

"LINGER LONGER IN LOVELY LUCAN" and "YOU CAN'T BEAT OUR MILK, BUT YOU CAN WHIP OUR CREAM," are two slogans from my boyhood village that have stuck with me for over half a century.

"LINGER LONGER IN LOVELY LUCAN" was displayed on the welcome sign at either end of the village. The slogan was coined by Isobel Haskett in the early 1950s as a result of a contest sponsored by the Lucan Lion's Club. "YOU CAN'T BEAT OUR MILK, BUT YOU CAN WHIP OUR CREAM" was printed on the back of Ivan Hearn's horse-drawn milk cart.

As a lad of fifteen, I worked for Hearn's Dairy in the summer of 1957. I delivered milk to the entire village, including stores, from a rubber-tired wagon pulled by a horse named Duke. Duke was no ordinary horse; he knew the milk route better than I— perhaps better than his owner, Ivan Hearn. Duke adored water puddles and would take off on a gallop as soon as he saw one. The challenge was always the same: How much dirty water could he splash into the wagon before I could close the

sliding doors? Duke won every time. I was forever wiping mud off the glass milk bottles.

Duke also had his favourite location to rid himself of his morning breakfast. This daily occurrence happened in front of Lankin's Shell Station. Without fail, as Duke was dropping his load, Jack Lankin, the owner, was handing me a shovel. Looking back on that great summer job, I often ask myself why Jack did not bag the stuff and sell it as garden fertilizer; he could have gathered tons of valuable manure.

Working for Hearn's Dairy had its perks. The route was divided into two, enabling the wagon to be reloaded. While this was being done, I had an open invitation to have breakfast each morning with the Hearn family, which soon became my favourite part of the day.

As Duke approached retirement at the age of fifteen, he was put out to pasture and replaced by a four-wheeled, rubber-tired, engine-driven, air-polluting truck.

In the words of the late Ivan Hearn, creamery owner, family man, hockey player, and reeve of Lucan: "Duke served his community well. His huge, powerful, white stature was an exciting symbol of a bygone day."

Scott's Elevator

During the Great Depression of the 1930s, the Clandeboye grain elevator burned to the ground. After salvaging what he could, owner Erwin Scott moved a few miles down the road to Lucan. In 1937, Scott purchased a grain elevator on William Street owned by the Hay Company and operated by Aaron Davis. The purchase came with several adjacent buildings across the road, including the former Western Hotel.

The Western Hotel had quite an illustrious past. It is believed that William Walker had the hotel constructed about 1860 during the time the Grand Trunk Railway built their line between Stratford and Sarnia. It became a well-known watering hole during the Donnelly era. The Donnellys themselves would have hoisted a few pints as they collected passengers for their stagecoach business from the nearby train station. In 1901, Bob Donnelly, a survivor of the 1880 massacre, and his nephew James Michael Donnelly purchased the hotel, which became known as the Donnelly House. In 1905, the Donnellys sold the hotel to John McFalls. The hotel ceased operating, it is believed, sometime during the First World War when prohibition was enacted. When Erwin Scott purchased the hotel, it had been empty for many years. He turned the structure into a chicken coop.

A progressive thinker with the foresight to expand his operation, Erwin Scott got into the turnip/rutabaga market, erecting another building to wash and wax the vegetables. Scott's trucks would head to the southern United States loaded with turnips and return to Lucan loaded with oranges and grapefruits. In those days, the village had its own government fruit and vegetable inspector. Joe Benn, a lifelong resident and farmer, was the man to ensure that consumer protection was upheld.

In addition to operating the grain elevator, Scott owned several farms throughout Biddulph and McGillivary Townships, where he grew seed grain. It was a natural transition for him to add a building for the sole purpose of cleaning and treating these crops. Proud of his agricultural products, he entered and won many prizes at London's Seed Fair held every March.

The Second World War brought with it new technology, including more sophisticated feeding systems. Scott's Elevator purchased a machine to mix concentrates with ground grain and another machine to mix molasses with cattle feed.

In the early years, the operation of a mill depended on the railroad, and Scott's Elevator was situated next to what had become the Canadian National line. Carloads of wheat and barley were shipped out from Scott's Elevator, as trainloads of feed grain were brought in from the Canadian Prairies. Four huge concrete silos were constructed to store the grain, and a modern seed-cleaning addition was installed. Scales capable of weighing trucks and wagons loaded with grain were assembled to take care of the expanding business.

To make room for the widening of William Street, Biddulph Township granted the London and Middlesex Historical Society first claim on the historic old Western Hotel. The plan was to move the building to Fanshawe Pioneer Village near London. When funds to make this costly move were not forthcoming, the old hotel was torn down. On the empty plot of land, an office and store complex was constructed, supplying the area farmers with livestock medicines, hardware, fencing supplies, work shoes, and clothes.

Erwin and Alice (Stewart) Scott were very active in the community. Erwin was the driving force for the construction of the Lucan Community Memorial Arena, becoming its first president. Their four children, Ruth, Donald, Douglas, and Alan all contributed to the running of the family business.

Alan and his son Mark operate Scott's Elevator today. Three generations of the Scott family praise the loyalty and dedication of their hard-working employees both past and present. Those employees have helped to make the family-owned and -operated business the success it has been for almost seventy years.

The derelict Western Hotel as it looked in 1960.

Scott's Elevator was established in 1937.

Wilberforce Inn

At the corner of Main and William Streets in Lucan's business district stands one of my favourite buildings. Today it houses the Wilberforce Inn, home to fine dining and bed and breakfast accommodation. When I was a child, that grand old building was our post office. I accompanied my dad whenever he picked up our mail. The walls of one room were lined with small, shiny brass letterboxes, rented by the villagers. You could tell by simply looking through the bevelled glass window on the door of your box if mail had been delivered. I derived great pleasure from peeking into those beautiful glass windows, checking everyone's mail status.

Records at the office of the Township of Lucan Biddulph indicate that the two-storey, red brick, V-shaped building was constructed in 1906. William Porte, Lucan's first postmaster (1859–96), had the structure built. When William retired, his son Fred W. Porte took over as postmaster for the next forty-seven years. Upon his retirement, Fred's sister Ida Kate Porte held the position of postmaster from 1943 to 1946. Thus, the Porte family operated the post office for over eighty years. In later years, the building became the office of Ed Unger's law practice, then the municipal office. With the amalgamation of the village of Lucan and Biddulph Township, they moved to a new, much larger, dwelling on the first of January 1999.

That same year, Irene and Tony Demas purchased the ninety-three-year-old building, spending thousands of dollars bringing the structure back to its original grandeur, providing class and elegance. The Demas family chose the name Wilberforce to honour Lucan's history, as the present-day village was originally called the Wilberforce Settlement.

The Wilberforce Inn opened in May of 2000. Tony and Irene offer romantic fireside dining in a Victorian-style ambience. The husband and wife team have been chefs and restaurateurs for three and a half decades. "We're extremely proud that our dining room offers a dining experience previously absent in Lucan," said Irene. The Wilberforce Inn's meals are exceptional and are always freshly prepared. Their wine cellar boasts 450 bottles, allowing the dinner guests a choice of over one hundred quality wines.

With a Bachelor of Science degree from the University of Western Ontario, son Anthony is now taking classes through the International Sommelier Guild with the intention of going through for his Masters of Wine while working at his parents' restaurant. When Stephanie, the youngest member of the Demas family, is not studying Arts Administration at the University of Ottawa, she is part of the Inn's staff as well. Stephanie has been heavily involved in the

Wilberforce Inn on Main Street.

London Theatre scene and has already produced two of her own plays.

"Lucan's tourism is on the rise because of the Donnelly tragedy, and we've had guests from Boston, California, and London, England. We had a wonderful couple named John and Nora Donnelly from County Offaly, Ireland, visit us in June of 2001. They had heard of the Donnelly saga and were intrigued not only by the Donnellys' link to Ireland, but also by their sharing of the same family name," Irene explained.

"With one guest suite and excellent food," said Tony, "we're hoping some of the tourists will make The Wilberforce Inn their overnight destination."

Visit their Web site,
www.wilberforceinn.com

Irene Demas in her wine cellar.

Manure as Renewable Energy

On CBC radio one morning in October of 2004, a newsreader spoke of a unique source of electricity produced from cattle manure. The story received my full attention when I learned that the farm discussed was located in Lucan.

Since the Walkerton, Ontario, tragedy of May 2000, the purity of our precious commodity, drinking water, remains a constant worry. That year, Walkerton's municipal water supply was contaminated by runoff from a livestock operation, causing a deadly strain of *E. coli* bacteria to infect the drinking water. Not only did hundreds of people become ill, seven died.

Lucan beef farmer Philip Lynn knows the importance of safety on the farm. Originally, Lynn had planned to create wetlands and spread the manure from his 5,500 head of beef cattle on the snow-covered fields during the winter months. Instead, he became involved in a massive program to produce 7,000 megawatt-hours of electricity per year. Seven thousand MWh is approximately the annual electricity demanded from 1,600 residential users, based on 350 KWh per user per month.

The Municipality of North Middlesex will use 2,500 MWh per year, becoming Canada's first green-powered municipality. Wes Hodgson, mayor of North Middlesex, says: "We will use the electricity to light, heat, and cool all the municipal buildings." Not only will the Lynn Farm produce 7,000 MWh of electricity, but it will also produce 9,000 metric tonnes of organic soil amendment/fertilizer.

According to Ontario Agriculture Minister Steve Peters, MPP for Elgin-Middlesex-London: "The Government of Ontario is firmly behind this project. Renewable energy from the farm is going to be an important part of this province's energy supply." The Ontario Government has given $1.6 million towards the renewable energy facility to be built on the Lynn Farm.

Philip Lynn has been researching and investigating methods of drying manure since 1999. Eventually he learned about biogas, and met Nils Semmler, president of RENTEC (Renewable Energy Technologies Incorporated). "Unlike the wind or the sun," said Semmler, "manure is a steady and predictable source of renewable power. The Lynn Farm produces sufficient manure volumes to easily demonstrate the viability of an Anaerobic Digestion (AD) system in Ontario. Lynn Farm has 100% control over all feed inputs because the farm has its own feed mill. The farm has established a consistent animal husbandry and manure-handling practice."

The project has multiple stakeholders, including Agriculture and Agri-Food Canada, Natural Resources Canada, the Ontario

Government, the Municipality of North Middlesex, Agricultural Adaption Council, Ontario Cattle Feeders' Association, and Trent University.

Beef farmer Philip Lynn says, "Donna Cansfield, the Ontario parliamentary assistant to Minister of Energy Dwight Duncan, deserves a lot of credit. She pushed the idea further and faster than anyone else." Donna Cansfield is quick to return the endorsement: "Philip Lynn demonstrates that wonderful entrepreneurial spirit that has always been a part of the farming community. When they have a problem, they wrestle with it, think outside the box, and solve the problem."

"Once operational," added Nils Semmler, "the farm-based plant will act as a model for facilitating widespread technology acceptance. The biogas project will create three full-time jobs and is hoped to be fully operational by the fall of 2006."

In our world of ever-increasing energy shortages, Philip Lynn's cattle operation is certainly a step towards bringing the rural farm back as a cornerstone of life.

Lucan beef farmer Philip Lynn knows the importance of safety on the farm.

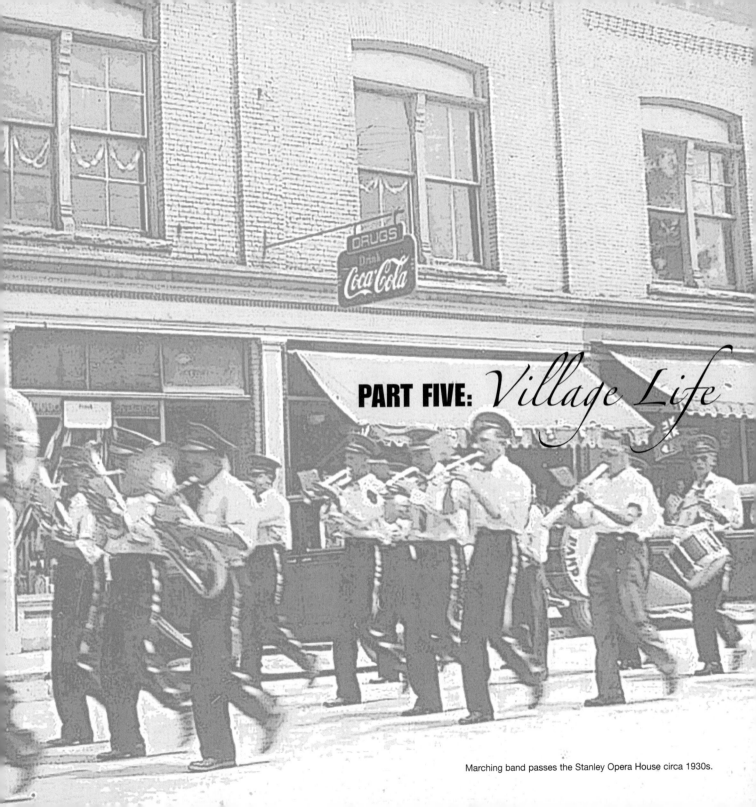

PART FIVE: *Village Life*

Marching band passes the Stanley Opera House circa 1930s.

Tollgates, Rail, and Storms

THE TOLL ROADS

At one point, the London to Goderich Road was maintained by tolls. Biddulph Township set up three tollgates to collect from the travelling public. Two were in Lucan at either end of the village, and the third was located a few miles to the north, in Mooresville. With a permit from the Township reeve, clergymen and funeral processions were allowed to pass through free at any time. Paying a toll at the first gate enabled stagecoaches to go straight through.

RATES OF TOLL:
One vehicle drawn by one horse – 7 cents
Each additional horse or other animal – 5 cents
A single horse, ridden, driven or led – 4 cents
Each head of horned cattle – 2 cents
Each score of sheep, hogs or less – 4 cents
Township residents passing through the gate once a day with vehicle and one horse – 3 cents
Each additional horse – 2 cents
For every single horse led, driven or ridden – 2 cents

Traffic on this road during the 1870s and 1880s was heavy. The tollgates became a nuisance for farmers, stagecoach drivers, and the travelling public. In March of 1882, a special meeting of the Biddulph and McGillivary township councils was held to discuss a ratepayers' petition to have the tolls abolished.

The first to go was the Mooresville tollgate. In 1884, the councils of Biddulph and Lucan ordered the two remaining gates removed after the merchants pointed out that their businesses were suffering. That same year, W.D. Stanley, warden of Middlesex County, succeeded in having all of the county tollgates removed. The only exceptions were those controlled by the Road Company on the Proof Line Road. They continued to operate, much to the dislike of the travelling public, until 1907.

RAILROAD FACTS

• The Stratford to Sarnia rail line was completed through Biddulph Township in 1859.
• During the 1880s, it was not uncommon for thirty trains a day to pass through Lucan, travelling between Stratford and Sarnia.
• The first Lucan station agent was J. H. Meagher, from Columbus, Nebraska.

- In 1887, the Lucan station agent sold 6,907 passenger tickets.
- Joe Murray was the last person to run a horse-drawn dray wagon collecting and delivering mailbags and freight from the station to the shopkeepers in the village. He ran his operation from 1923 to 1951.
- The last freight train ran between St. Marys and Lucan in December of 1989.

By 1878, rail compared to stagecoach travel proved to be a lot faster for mail and freight delivery and a lot more comfortable for passengers. That same year, the stagecoach line between London and Goderich ceased to exist, although the run between Lucan and London continued. One of the drivers was John Casper (Cap) Howard. "I was perched on top of the stagecoach for many a cold winter run," claimed Cap, "often wishing I had chosen an occupation with less cold weather attached." Cap Howard had a reputation as one of the best stage drivers, in the days when roads, not traffic, presented a hazard. It was said of Cap that if anyone could get through difficult terrain, he could.

With the advent of the horseless motorbus, Cap Howard learned a new form of driving. He became the only stagecoach driver to switch from horsepower to gasoline-powered engine. Each weekday, Cap drove his truck-like bus from Lucan to London and back. The tin-roofed vehicle with side curtains to protect the passengers from the elements was a rough ride caused by solid rubber tires. The headlamps were lit from a propane tank mounted on the running board.

In 1937, Western Ontario Motorways bought Cap's bus franchise. Nine years later, on the advice of his doctor, he retired for a well-earned rest.

FIERCE STORMS RECALLED

NOVEMBER 9th, 1913

A terrible blizzard swept across the Great Lakes, taking with it the lives of sailors as it destroyed their ships. In the Lucan area, trains were stalled in snowdrifts, telephone and telegraph service was knocked out, and whiteouts made the roads impassable.

JANUARY 26th, 1971

I vividly remember the horrendous snowstorm of 1971. I was a twenty-nine-year-old news cameraman at CFPL Television in London when the blizzard hit. Twenty-eight-year-old reporter George Clark and I were assigned to go as far north as we could in order to bring a story back for the six o'clock news program. The Ontario Provincial Police were turning back motorists heading north on Highway 4 at Masonville, but allowed the two of us in our marked news cruiser to pass. We soon realized that driving was a nightmare. Cars and snowplows were abandoned at the side of the highway. Drifting snow and poor visibility made it almost impossible to stay on the road. We were crawling along for what seemed a very long time. Finally, we were able to make out a gas station/restaurant to our right and we pulled in. Although relieved to find shelter, we were surprised to find ourselves among some eighty other motorists, all stranded.

Over the next twenty-four hours, the folks operating the smoke-filled diner ran out of food, and the one and only washroom was no longer functional, unable to hold up to prolonged use. On the morning of the second day, reporter Clark learned that all of the students at St Patrick's School on the Roman Line were snowbound. That afternoon, with our film camera, microphone, and new friend Bill Marshall, we set off on foot hoping to reach the school. Bill Marshall, a Toronto documentary producer, was on his way to Sarnia to visit Orlo Miller, author of the book *The Donnellys Must Die*. Marshall was hoping to persuade Miller to turn the book into a movie.

As the three of us stumbled along, the howling wind slowed our progress and the whipping snow almost blinded us. At times we thought we could hear sounds of transport trucks heading in our direction. It was a frightening experience. Just when we thought we couldn't go any farther, we noticed the snowy outline of a farmhouse to our right. With renewed energy, we made our way along a snow-covered lane. The farm couple invited us into their home, offering hot soup and freshly baked bread. It tasted heavenly. We learned that their children were among the many pupils stranded at St. Patrick's school.

Before we ventured back out into the elements, the farmer took one look at George's stylish loafers and supplied him with a good pair of winter boots. Warm inside and out, we trudged north, eventually making it to the school on the Roman Line. The children were all in good spirits, making the best of a potentially bad situation. As darkness fell, a snowplow arrived at the school, followed by a school bus filled with hot food and blankets. The students could not be returned to their respective farm homes until the following day, as the rural roads were just being cleared. George, Bill, and I hitched a ride to Lucan with the returning bus.

The driver let us off at the door to the Canadian Legion hall, and within minutes, as tired as we were, we were sipping beer and eating the finest pickled eggs we had ever tasted. The roads to London were still impassable, and we did not have a place to stay. Ivan Hearn generously invited the three of us to stay overnight at his home. Ivan and his wife, Kit, have been lifelong friends. He was the owner of Hearn's Dairy and the reeve of Lucan. Their generosity extended to loaning us a car the next morning, enabling us to return to London.

The big storm of 1971 had been quite an adventure for many, including Premier John Robarts, who was stranded at a 401 Service Centre near Woodstock. Over twenty-four inches of snow fell, with drifts piled up along some roadways as high as twelve feet.

MARCH 1976

The London weather office measured ice two inches thick coating upright objects after a twenty-four-hour freezing rainstorm. Many trees and power lines crashed to the ground. Some homeowners were without hydro for seven days.

Television footage of CFPL TV reporter George Clark and documentary maker Bill Marshall as they trek from Elginfield to St. Patrick's school during the snowstorm of January 26th, 1971.

W.H. Lambourn became Lucan's new C.N.R. agent in 1961.

John Casper 'Cap' Howard, a former stagecoach driver, retires from his mail delivery route.

Ghost of McIlhargy's Tavern

Researching this book, I was always made to feel welcome at my Aunt Muriel Culbert's house on Francis Street in Lucan. One morning at breakfast, Aunt Muriel asked if I'd heard of the ghost of McIlhargy's Tavern. I had not, and she proceeded to tell me the fascinating story, as she knew it.

The original building still stands today. I've always known that attractive brick house on the southern outskirts of the village simply as the Brownlee home. It was built by Patrick McIlhargy during the summer of 1850. Its function was to be a welcome hotel and pub for thirsty, tired men and women travelling on the sixty-mile stretch known as the London–Goderich Road. The dwelling consisted of a large kitchen, dining room, and bar on one side. Located across the hall was a surgery and waiting room run by Patrick's son, Doctor John McIlhargy. Accommodation for travellers and a large ballroom for dancing were situated on the second floor. Squire Patrick McIlhargy was also a justice of the peace, a Catholic, and a long-time friend of the Donnelly family. Several inquests were held in the upstairs ballroom, including the inquest into the death of Patrick Farrell at the hands of James Donnelly Sr.

My curiosity was piqued and I set out to visit the ghost house. For the past three decades, the owner has been Leslie Carling-Lindsay.

Leslie welcomed me into her home, and as we sat at the kitchen table sipping coffee, a menagerie of family pets joined us. Misty, a twenty-pound Siamese feline, and Shadow, a cockapoo canine, curiously eyed me. In addition there was Sunny, a longhaired collie, and perched in a cage was a very noisy, thirty-year-old cockatoo called Sam. This tiny, talkative bird proceeded to squawk with great gusto, forcing me to click off my tape recorder a number of times. None of this deterred or slowed down Leslie. She proceeded to tell me the very interesting history of this old house.

In 1978, Leslie and her husband, Keith Lindsay, purchased McIlhargy's Tavern from Marg and Charlie Elson. When the Elsons mentioned a ghost living in the house, Leslie was horrified. However, Charlie Elson was quick to laugh it off and spoke about squirrels rolling nuts around in the attic. Leslie somewhat reluctantly accepted the story, and the house deal was finalized.

It did not take Leslie long to realize that the ghost story was not a laughing matter and had some substance to it. By way of explanation, Leslie got up from the kitchen table and walked across the room to an old door leading to the parlour. Placing her hand on the door, she said: "When the latch is tightly clicked shut, the door is not supposed to open. Imagine my horror when all of a sudden while sitting in the kitchen, I observed the latch being lifted and the door creaking open.

"That was not the only incident. There were other occurrences. Many times, going up or down the stairs to the second floor, I could feel something brush past me. It was so palpable, it gave me the shivers! At the time that my youngest son Gordon was a baby, a rocking chair in his bedroom would constantly move. I could clearly hear the creaking noise while watching television downstairs. I eventually got rid of the chair. Gordon's cradle also sat on a rocker-base. Every time I laid Gordon into the cradle, it started to rock and would not stop. These were my first experiences with something strange and unexplainable taking place in our home.

"Another time, I hired a carpenter to do some repair work after a small interior fire. The man was left on his own while we went shopping in nearby London. Upon our return, the carpenter seemed quite upset. He finally asked me somewhat sheepishly if we had spirits in the house. I told him yes, but no one had ever seen a ghost. 'Well I saw her,' he claimed. His voice trembled as he went on to describe his experience on the stairs. 'I saw someone standing at the top of the stairs and at first didn't think much of it because I've seen so many people coming and going in this house. Then, a few moments later, this apparition swooped by me. I couldn't move. I was rooted to the spot. She was grey in colour and was wearing an old-fashioned dress covered with a long grey skirt. Everything was grey, including her skin,' he told me. 'I was really terrified!' After hearing that story from our carpenter, we have always referred to the ghost as the 'Grey Lady,'" Leslie explained.

Years later, Leslie divorced Keith and met Ted McKenzie. "I had the distinct feeling the Grey Lady didn't like Ted, as she was constantly locking him out of the house. I've always felt the reason was because we were remodelling, changing her familiar surroundings, and she blamed it on Ted. I remember sitting right here at the kitchen table as Ted passed me on his way to the back garden. When he tried to re-enter the house, the door had mysteriously locked. This happened a number of times. Fortunately, after we finished our restoration, the Grey Lady settled down and has not been observed since. This is much to Ted's relief," Leslie said, smiling. "And as for myself, after my initial fear and apprehension, I have come to tolerate and accept the Grey Lady. I dare say I miss her a little bit."

McIlhargy's Tavern

Poplar Farm

At the time the third house was built on the Culbert homestead, my great-grandfather Richard Culbert planted dozens of poplar trees on either side of the driveway leading from the road to his new home. Those same trees are still standing today, silent witnesses to the first Irish settlers and their descendants.

My pioneer ancestors immigrated to Biddulph Township in 1840, from the small farming community of Ballymackey, County Tipperary, in Ireland. My great-great-grandparents John and Mary (Ward) Culbert set sail for Upper Canada with three small children and John's father, William. At that time, the Irish were immigrating to the New World in great numbers to escape poverty, disease, and hunger. The voyage was often difficult. John and Mary were struck a blow when their youngest child and John's father died during the six-week voyage.

Heartbroken and distraught, they considered returning to Ireland. However, after the sailing vessel docked in Halifax, Nova Scotia, John learned about the Canada Company's sale of land in an area known as the Queen's Bush, north of London. Mary and John decided to press on. They purchased a team of horses and a wagon, setting out on their strenuous trek over rough and difficult trails. With a lot of prayers and a bit of luck, they safely arrived at their destination.

On the 10th of October 1840, John and Mary purchased 100 acres of land on Concession Two, later known as the Coursey Line. They paid the Canada Company sixty-two pounds, ten shillings for the timber-covered property, and after that the hard work began. John unendingly cut down trees to give them space and provide material to build a log cabin. As soon as they had prepared a workable farm, John and Mary bought some livestock, and farming began in earnest.

Over the next thirteen years, my great-great-grandmother Mary Culbert would bear ten more children. A larger, more comfortable log house was erected farther back from the road. Richard, the youngest of the children, was born in the second log home in 1853. He would eventually inherit the farm. At the age of twenty-six, my great-grandfather Richard married Jane Eleanor Fairhall. On the 23rd of February 1881, Jane gave birth to a daughter named Hulda May. Over the next few years, five more children were born: Myron (my grandfather), Lela, Arthur, Mary, and Ethel. A hard-working and dependable couple, Richard and Jane were well liked and respected by their neighbours. Richard, a proud citizen, was a Tory and an Orangeman. The only two framed pictures on the walls of their log cabin were of Queen Victoria and William of Orange.

During the mid-1890s, Richard decided he needed a more substantial home for his family. A few yards south of the log cabin, he dug out the basement by hand, and cut enough timber to frame the entire house. Richard hired a local contractor and paid him just under a thousand dollars for the construction of his house. The family moved into their new home in 1895. It was at that point that Richard planted the avenue of poplar trees, hence the name Poplar Farm.

After many years of farming, Richard and Jane retired to nearby Lucan. They bought a small home where they kept a cow, a few pigs, a small flock of chickens, and a vegetable patch. I never knew my great-grandfather Richard. He died in 1932, ten years before I was born. I do remember his wife, my great-grandmother Jane. She was a tiny, cheerful woman in her nineties, constantly knitting socks for her great-grandchildren, including me.

When my grandfather Myron Manford Culbert took over Poplar Farm from his parents, he married Effie Pearl Taylor. They had six children, all boys, who were named: Clifford, Kenneth, Ivan, Milward (my father, who was called Mel), Merton, and Earl.

Prior to my birth, my grandfather Myron slipped and fell from the barn roof, severely damaging both his knees. He walked on crutches for the remainder of his life. Even with his severe handicap, grandfather Myron continued to work his farm. Such was the tenacity of that generation.

My memories of Poplar Farm are rich and numerous. At a 2004 family get-together, I made a request of the attendees to share a few farm memories for this book. Although my grandparents and their six sons have all passed away, I was honoured to receive notes from my three surviving aunts, some first cousins, and my two sisters.

Aunt Helen Culbert of Calgary, Alberta, who was married to Ken:

My mother-in-law, Effie, kept a well-run house. Monday was laundry day and everything had to be ironed, including the bedding. On Wednesday, she baked. She canned her own jams and pickles and churned her own butter. It was wonderful!

One Christmas, as the story goes, Effie was making her annual non-alcoholic raspberry wine. My husband, Ken, was a boy at the time, and had received a recipe from a friend at school that included yeast. A few days later, Ken's father smelled something peculiar in the summer kitchen. After Myron discovered it was moonshine, Ken was punished in the woodshed with the strap.

Now that I am an old lady, I realize how hard my mother-in-law worked. They were wonderful grandparents to my sons Cam and Greg. God bless them both!

Poplar Farm in the early 1900s.

Terry Culbert's Lucan ~ Home of the Donnellys

A large gathering of the Culbert clan posing for a snapshot in November of 2004.

Richard and Jane Culbert with their six grown children, Hulda May, Myron (my grandfather), Lela, Arthur, Mary, and Ethel.

My grandparents Myron and Effie Culbert

Effie and Myron with their son Ivan. "This was the day I told my mother and dad I had joined the army, and I was leaving for England that same night. Six years and four months later, I rejoined them."

Aunt Gladys Culbert of Strathroy, Ontario, who was married to Cliff:

I remember fondly the family gatherings on special occasions. In the winter, the snow was not always cleared along the Coursey Line, so Myron would meet us at Highway 4 with a sleigh and a team of horses to transport us to the farm. After a wonderful meal and when the dishes were done, we would all go into the parlour, where Effie played the piano for a singalong. Those were wonderful times!

Aunt Muriel Culbert of Lucan, Ontario, who was married to Mert:

As a young woman, I dated Mert, a friend of my brother's. One bright but chilly Sunday afternoon, Mert and I decided to go for a drive in the country. At nineteen years of age, I was looking forward to spending a couple of hours alone with Mert and also showing off my new fur coat. As we travelled the back roads, I mentioned to him that I must get home to help prepare dinner for my family of ten. Passing the old Hudson place where my father kept cattle, Mert began to slow down. Before I knew it, he was turning up the long tree-lined driveway to his parents' farm.

"Where are we going? I asked.

"I have to see my mother for a moment," was his reply.

"Take me home first," I told him, but he wasn't listening.

"I'll only be a second," he said as he raced to the house.

Moments later, there was a tapping on the window of the car. His mother, Effie, smiled at me and insisted that I come in. Once inside the cozy farmhouse, I was greeted by Mert's father, Myron, Mert's older brother, Mel, and Mel's wife, Mary [the author's parents]. From the corner of my eye, I could see there was an extra place setting at the table, and then it dawned on me that this whole drive in the country was a scam, so that I could meet Mert's family!

On the way home that evening, I asked Mert why he had not mentioned the dinner invitation to me. With one hand on the steering wheel and his other in mine, Mert smiled his boyish smile and said, " I didn't think you would come!"

Cousin Campbell Culbert of Fulbrook, Oxfordshire, England, eldest son of Ken and Helen:

I remember Grampa swinging off his crutches onto the driver's seat of his Model-T Ford. He had pushed the seat back on its rails as far as it would go, enabling his rigid legs to fit under the dashboard. With a length of binder twine attached to the choke, he'd chug down the

Coursey Line to the creamery in Lucan, silver milk cans clanging on the rack he'd built above the back bumper.

I remember the kitchen table covered with country crockery, serving dishes steaming with vegetables, platters of meat, preserves, and pies. Grampa always said grace before we ate and often read a lesson from the United Church publication, *The Upper Room*.

We played games in a barnboard teepee our uncles had built for us. I remember the pond, sucking mud, cow-crowded, heat, and endless sky. In the winter, flooded fields, frozen, skating miles through stubble. In the house, rag rugs—the final resting place of worn-out dungarees, overalls, and suits, relieved by a little colour. But, that red? Surely not Gramma Effie's? And no, never knickers?

The outhouse, Eatons and Simpsons catalogues, waste not, nor linger on the lingerie? Cousins locking each other in, playing dirty tricks. The kittens we blasted with hot milk straight from the udder, knocking them off their hind feet, blinking and licking and coming back for more. And so did we all, and so did we all. Thank you, Myron and Effie.

Cousin Greg Culbert of Calgary, Alberta, second son of Ken and Helen and brother of Campbell:

Cam and I always loved to help feed the chickens and collect the eggs still warm in the laying boxes. Grandma would look carefully at each egg against a strong light bulb and grade for size, and I can remember her joy when she would discover a "double-yolker." They apparently brought more money at the time of sale.

I never knew Grandpa before his fall from the barn roof. His handicap never seemed to get in his way. He was a wonderful gardener and if he wasn't leaning on one crutch hoeing, he would be flat out on a belly box he'd made, enabling him to get right down with his plants.

The root cellar was a scary place. Lit by a few bare light bulbs, it had a heavy and sweet smell produced from great bins of apples, potatoes, carrots, and onions. The whitewashed walls were lined with shelves, stocked with preserves in quart sealers. One winter, when I was three or four, and it was too cold to go to the outhouse, Grandma took me to the cellar and placed me on an old oak chair with arms, which had been modified as a toilet. As I sat there, the silhouette of a mouse appeared on the floor. I

The author and his cousins Greg and Cam catching insects in the front garden.

My uncle Mert with his son Mike and my father Mel in the sheep pen.

shouted for Grandma as the mouse scampered into the darkness. Back upstairs, Grandma picked up Fluffy the cat, took her to the basement door and told her that she had work to do. In the morning, Grandma was presented with a trophy. Petting Fluffy's head, Grandma buried the poor little dead mouse in the lacy fern pot that sat on a table underneath the crank telephone. Grandma claimed the success she had with her houseplants was due to the buried mice planted in her flowerpots.

I have very fond memories of Poplar Farm. It was a place of great adventure, and I often wonder how my life would have played out if my father had stayed in Lucan.

My sister Dana Garrett of London, Ontario, daughter of Mel and Mary:

Cousin Marilyn and I were about six years of age when our parents let us go on an overnight visit to Poplar Farm. We called it our holiday. Our bedroom seemed enormous, with a lot of room to run around and hide in. There was no bathroom in the house, so it became quite an adventure to use the "thunder-mug" located under the bed. Across the hallway was another bedroom, its only window filled with bees. That was very frightening for two small girls!

I remember Grandpa being very strict and Grandma loving us in her own way. She was always busy and didn't have a lot of time to spend with us, although she kept a close eye on what we were doing. Grandma had beautiful formal gardens at the front of the house, with rows upon rows of flowers you could walk through. Her hollyhocks dwarfed Marilyn and me. We always thought of our overnight visits to the farm as an adventure; it felt as if we were far away from our families in Lucan. In reality, we were only three miles down the road.

Cousin Phil Culbert of Vernon, British Columbia, son of Ivan and Elvira:

What I remember about Poplar Farm are the stories Dad told us as children. Most of those tales were about how he and his five brothers got into trouble with their father. One winter's day after a fresh snowfall, Dad and his older brother Cliff decided to take the horses out of the barn and hitch them to the sleigh. Without permission from their father, Myron, the two lads had planned to joyride through the snow-covered fields. For some reason, the harnesses became loose and the horses took off, only to be found hours later by Grandpa in a far-away neighbour's field. At that evening's dinner table, Ivan and Cliff found it difficult to sit on their posteriors.

My favourite picture is one taken of my dad in his army uniform, standing between Grandma and Grandpa in front of the farmhouse. No one in the picture is smiling; in fact, each face tells a different story. Dad's is a look of excitement and anxiousness. Grandpa's is a look of absolute pride, and Grandma's look, with her dark sunken eyes, was that of great consternation. On the back of the picture in my father's handwriting were the following words: "This was the day I told my Mother and Father I had joined the army, and I was leaving for England that same night. Six years and four months later, I rejoined them." The picture was dated January 20th, 1940.

My sister Mary Jane Culbert of Vancouver, British Columbia, daughter of Mel and Mary:

"Let's see . . . it should be just about here!" Uncle Mert stepped onto the tread of the staircase leading to the upstairs bedrooms. Creak! "That's it!"

This was the single stair that the Culbert boys tried so hard to avoid. Uncle Mert told me how he and his brothers would come home late after a wild night in old Lucan town and try to creep silently up the staircase to bed. That one creaking stair spelled doom if they stepped on it and woke their parents.

Stories like these came alive when Uncle Mert took me to visit Poplar Farm in the 1990s. I have no early memories of the farm nor do I remember my father, Mel (Uncle Mert's favourite brother). My father died at the age of thirty-eight, when I was only a year old. Uncle Mert painted a vivid picture in my mind of life on Poplar Farm with my father, my five uncles, and my grandparents.

Members of my family and those connected to Poplar Farm cherish all of the above memories.

In 1953, my grandparents Myron and Effie retired from the farm and moved into Lucan. Their fifth-born son, Mert, his wife, Muriel, and her brother Harry Hardy bought the property. In 1958, Mert and Muriel sold their half of the farm to Harry, closing a 118-year chapter of Culbert history on the Coursey Line. In 1969, Harry severed three acres surrounding the house from the original hundred acres. The three acres and house were sold to Vincent Venile, who lived on the property until 1976.

That same winter, Donna Wells discovered Poplar Farm. She was driving along the Coursey Line searching for a barn to sketch when she came across the "For Sale" sign. It was love at first sight. Not long after that discovery, Donna and her husband, Joe, bought Poplar Farm. Renovations took place over the next few years, restoring the stately residence to its former glory. Their children, Martha, Sarah, and Jonathan, were excited about the adventure of living in the country. With a long interest in anything equestrian, the family was now able to have their horses close at hand.

The Wells's love of horses led to their holding many fox hunts over the years. The Trollope Hunt and the Wellington Waterloo Hunt Club were frequent guests. "The generous co-operation of our many neighbours allowed us to hold the hunts," recalls Donna. "We sometimes had seventy-five horses and riders taking part, with forty hounds, who could hunt for five or six hours and not ever run out of land, which meant that we never caught a fox. Life in the country, entertaining countless guests, and appreciating the rich past of the property are just some of the blessings and pleasures we've received at Poplar Farm."

**Donna and Joe Wells bought
Poplar Farm in 1976.**

Goodison Steam Thresher

The John Goodison Thresher Company was established in 1881 in Sarnia, Ontario. In the thirteenth year of operation, president John Goodison wrote these words in his annual Goodison Machinery catalogue: *To our Customers and Friends, the threshermen and farmers of the Dominion. Goodison Machinery is the result of years of practical experience and gradual improvement, and no change of any kind is made until it has been thoroughly tested and known to be an improvement. On the judgment of the threshermen, in the field or barn, any threshing devices must stand or fall, and much of what has been achieved towards the perfection of threshing machinery is due to this discriminating judgment. In the construction of this thresher we spare neither time nor money to make it the simplest and most durable and economical of threshing machines.*

The first threshing machines run by steam were built in the early nineteenth century. Even though those early machines were cumbersome and heavy, they were a great improvement over working a farm by horses only. The average farm in those days was 100 acres, and a farmer with a walking plow and horse walked eight miles per acre. The first thresher still required horsepower. To separate wheat and other crops of grain from the chaff, the thresher was powered by a power sweep, turned by horses.

In the United States, the first "self-propelled" steam engine was built in 1855, twenty-six years before the John Goodison Thresher Company was established. The problem with the new machine was that it did not have a steering mechanism and still needed horses to change direction. In 1880, a steering device was finally patented, and shortly thereafter, the clutch was invented. With steam pressures now reaching 150 psi, work on the farm became a bit easier. Horses were still needed to draw water, wood, or coal to fuel the boiler.

Steam production declined in the early twentieth century. In 1924, a gas-powered tractor called the Farmall was doing everything the steam engine could do, only faster and more efficiently. The Second World War saw steam production come to a stop. Today, just a few of these marvellous old machines are still around. They are mostly found at antique tractor shows.

When Doug Ovens, a Biddulph Township farmer, spotted a 1925 John Goodison steam engine at an auction, he knew he had to have it. Doug gets excited talking about the engine he purchased in 1998. "After all, it was steam that opened up our country. Steamships brought us

Biddulph Township farmer Doug Ovens and his #2506 John Goodison Steam Thresher, built in Sarnia, Ontario, in 1925.

produce and steam trains connected Canada. Steam is what made our country what it is today!" explains Doug. Old #2506 was Canadian-built by the John Goodison Thresher Company Limited. There were only three of this particular model built, and Doug owns the only machine remaining in the world.

A lot of work has gone into refurbishing the steam thresher to its original splendour. Doug takes his prize possession to steam shows throughout Ontario, hauling the enormous machine on a tandem float trailer pulled by a powerful truck. He claims that old-timers in their eighties and nineties are instantly jolted back to their younger years when they observe the engine fired up, see the plumes of wood smoke, and hear the shrill sound of the steam whistle.

"They see history brought to life," Doug said. "They love to roll up their sleeves and feed a pitchfork or two of grain to the threshing machine. No thoughts of aches and pains—this is a regular fountain of youth. Not only do the older folks get a kick out of this machine, but it is also a great educational tool for young people. They are amazed to watch a piece of equipment designed almost a century ago that is still operational."

Doug's engine weighs twelve tonnes. In Western Canada, larger machines weighing up to twenty tonnes were used for plowing. "Imagine seventy-five years ago, one of those large machines on the Prairies pulling a twenty-furrow plow, operating on nothing more than wood and water. I remember when I was a boy watching these massive machines move from one farm to the next. It was quite exciting to see a steam engine and water wagon coming along a country gravel road; nothing quite compared to that. Machinery was so much simpler then. Farmers did all of their own repairs and if they couldn't afford to buy a part, they made the part. If a drive-belt broke, you simply slit the belt with a knife, laced it together, and it kept right on going. Today we have vehicles and tractors we cannot repair ourselves, because computers run everything. It sure makes you appreciate the knowledge our forefathers had and how ingenious they were!"

During the summer of 2004, Doug and his Goodison Steam Thresher were invited to the National Threshers Association Sixtieth Anniversary Reunion in Wauseon, Ohio. He took along his portable Robert Bell Steam Engine as well. The smaller engine was built in 1948 in Seaforth, Ontario. "They treated me like royalty in the United States. It was a real honour to be part of that show, which is the largest of its kind in North America," he said.

Doug received his biggest compliment when the picture of his beloved #2506 made it onto the front cover of the 2006 National Threshers Association Reunion brochure.

The Farm Boy

As a boy, Harry Hardy loved going anywhere his father would take him. On a warm spring morning in 1938, his dad asked him to help bring home a herd of cattle from a farm situated between Parkhill and Ailsa Craig. After the cattle were rounded up and out on the main road, his father looked at him and said: "You drive them home, Son!"

"But Dad," said the young boy, "I don't know the way!"

"Well you can ask," his father said sternly, as he got in his car and drove away.

Frightened and bewildered, the eight-year-old boy drove the herd of thirty massive animals down the road towards Lucan. Three times Harry had to stop and ask directions. He recalls the first farmer he talked to being horrified at the sight of a lone child herding all those beef cattle by himself. "Where's your dad?" asked the farmer.

"He left for home," said Harry.

"Where's your mother?"

"She's at home working," Harry answered.

"Where's your brothers and sisters?"

"They're doing other chores."

The astonished farmer looked at the herd, then back at Harry as he lifted his arm, pointing: "Lucan's that way, Son!"

"This is what you were expected to do when growing up as a farm boy. I never lost any of those cattle on that fifteen-mile walk. That was my first introduction to cattle driving and over the years I became very good at that job. When I think of my grandson at eight years of age, I still find it hard to believe that my father had me driving cattle on my own. More than likely nowadays, I'll get a call from my kids to come and babysit their eight-year-old. Times certainly have changed."

In March of 1943, Harry's parents ran out of water at the farm. His father began drawing water from a property across the road. "Pulled by Nell, our old grey mare," said Harry, "we transported the water in a large wooden barrel on top of a stone boat. To keep the water from splashing out, Dad placed an old door over the barrel and I sat on it. On one trip back to our farm, an edge of the stone boat hit a protruding rock, knocking the door and me flying to the ground. Even though I hurt my knee, I jumped back up, and away we went, not wasting any time.

"The following morning, I was to go with my father to see some cattle. By then I was feeling poorly and told Dad I was unable to go. He knew right away that something was wrong; I never missed an opportunity to accompany him. Dad called Doctor Banting, our family doctor. After checking the swelling on my leg, he said: "I think he has osteomyelitis, but I'm not sure.

I've only had one case like this before, and she died!"

That diagnosis was indeed frightening news for the Hardy family. They watched young Harry lie in bed in a delirious state for the next three weeks. Doctor Murray Simpson of London was summoned to the farm, and Harry was immediately rushed to St. Joseph's Hospital. "For three days, I ran a temperature of 106 and three-fifths [106.6]," said Harry. "The doctors wouldn't allow Dad to leave the hospital, fearing that I would be dead before he reached his car."

The fever finally broke, and the tall, lanky thirteen-year-old was ready to be prepared to undergo the necessary operation on his leg. Harry's brother Jack decided to smuggle one of Harry's racing pigeons into the hospital to keep Harry company. The only person who knew about this winged patient under Harry's bed was Sister Bernadine, and she kept the secret between the two of them.

The morning of Harry's operation, two nurses came into his room to inform him that the surgery had been cancelled. "In those days, a telephone call between London and Lucan was long distance and only to be made in an emergency. Knowing that my mother had planned the long trip to the hospital later that day, I was desperate to let her know about the cancellation. I decided to send her a note via airmail," chuckled Harry. "One of the nurses wrote the note, I rolled it up, placing it in a tiny aluminium tube. When I told them about the winged patient under my bed, they laughed as they retrieved the bird while I attached the band to its leg. The faithful homing pigeon winged its way towards Lucan."

To Harry's great surprise, half an hour later his mom appeared at his bedside. He knew his pigeon was a fast racer, but he also knew that it was impossible to reach Lucan in such a short time. Of course, there was a simple explanation. Mrs. Hardy had accepted a lift from friends, not realizing an important airmail message was making its way to her home. In the meantime, Harry enjoyed his mom's unexpected visit.

I have known Harry Hardy all my life. He never tires of sharing his farm stories. He can hold court at any gathering, keeping his audience enthralled for hours, and have them come back for more.

Thirteen-year-old Harry Hardy.

Slingshot and Fishing Rod

My friend Harold Frost loved the outdoors so much that he spent his entire working career with the Ontario Government's Forestry Division in Northern Ontario. Now retired, Harold and his wife, Pierrette, live in the Huron County town of Clinton. Wood is still Harold's passion, only now it is expressed through woodworking. I sat with the Frosts in their beautiful new home and talked of Harold's childhood growing up in Lucan.

"My earliest memories are going fishing at the age of seven with my older brother, Keith, along the banks of the Little Ausable River. We always caught at least one fish to bring home to eat," Harold said. "Keith and I were pretty lucky and regularly caught pike and shiners, and rock and smallmouth bass, to the delight of our mother.

"As I grew older, I began to hunt with a slingshot. It didn't take me long to become a pretty good marksman. Rabbits were my usual target, and our family always enjoyed a good meal of rabbit stew or rabbit pie. Sooner or later, my skill with the slingshot would get me into trouble. I remember being on a school field trip on the outskirts of Lucan when our teacher spotted a blackbird perched high in a tree on the riverbank. Without giving it a second thought, I whipped my slingshot from my back pocket, took aim and knocked the bird off the branch. Carl Crocker, our teacher, was annoyed, but my classmates sure were impressed."

Another slingshot episode occurred when Harold was fourteen. He and Tom (Hooley) Brooks were walking near the village garbage dump on the Coursey Line. "We were fooling around, shooting pebbles at tin cans, glass bottles, and at each other. At one point Hooley hollered: 'You can't hit me!' Never shying away from a challenge, I took aim, fired, and hit him right on the end of the nose, skinning him between his eyes. I came that close to a potential disaster. I'll never forget that day. We were both really scared. It certainly taught us a lesson—at least for a little while."

Harold and his brother Keith have always been daredevils. I remember during recess at public school, watching the two of them scramble to the top of the old maple trees behind the school. "I got a kick out of chasing Keith from tree to tree," Harold said, "as our friends cheered us on from down below. It was a real adrenaline rush. Searching for other tree adventures, we spent many hours in Cecil Hodgins' bush. Keith and I would climb twenty to thirty feet up to the top of the smaller trees and our body weight would bend them over, bringing us back to the ground without getting out of the tree. What a sight for anyone passing by!

"Did I ever get hurt? You bet! Did that stop me? No way! Once I fell out of an apple tree and split my head open, which was a very painful experience. Another time I was hunting pigeons in a barn with Harvey Hayes. I climbed a ladder to block a hole so the pigeons couldn't fly out. From this vantage point, I discovered a platform. As I stepped onto it, a loud cracking sound filled the cavernous barn as the platform gave way. Falling, I grabbed a track above me and hung on for dear life. Suspended in mid-air, I could see Harvey standing a long way below me. He was holding a flashlight, looking as frightened as I was because he couldn't think of anything to help me in my precarious position. Finally, the strength in my arms gave way, sending my body hurtling towards the barn floor. I was knocked unconscious. I learned later that Harvey had run to a nearby farmer for help. While I was still out for the count, the farmer lifted me into his car and as he raced towards St. Joseph's Hospital in London, he stopped to pick up my mother in Lucan. I regained consciousness as we entered the emergency department. I had been out cold for two hours. After the doctors examined me, they discovered a broken arm and a cracked pelvis. My stay in the hospital lasted a full month. At a follow-up examination, the doctors discovered that my arm hadn't healed properly. They were forced to re-break the arm and wire it up again. I was in a cast once more for another month."

At the age of thirteen, Harold's devil-may-care attitude finally caught up with him. He received an injury that left him scarred for life.

Seven-year-old Harold (1947), fishing in the Ausable River.

As he tells the tale: "We had divided into two groups, battling each other as boys are known to do. The odd time, someone would get slightly hurt, but for the most part we had great fun.

"My group was hanging out behind Clarence Lewis's Barber Shop while the other group hid in McFall's barn. We were shooting at each other with slingshots and air rifles, fully engrossed in the battle to win. I thought I was very clever when I decided to hide behind the barber's new car. No one would dare shoot towards the automobile and potentially mark it. However, Terry Hodgins had no such scruples. He spotted me, aimed and hit me in the eye with a pellet from his air rifle. I remember feeling excruciating pain and not being able to see at all.

I was convinced I was about to go blind. After another hospital emergency run, I still had my sight, albeit somewhat blurry. I was sent home wearing an eye patch. Thankfully, I didn't lose my sight but I have suffered permanent eye damage."

Harold's drive for adventure has substantially mellowed over the years, but his love for trees has never waned. He continues to be involved in woodlot management and has painstakingly completed all of the carpentry work in his new home. His wife, Pierette, is especially pleased about the large art studio Harold has built for her.

Harold at sixteen, with a snowy owl found in Shipley's farm field.

Beware of Bovines

Bruce Currie was a fortunate little boy who had two sets of living grandparents. His paternal grandparents, the Curries, lived in Nova Scotia, while his maternal grandparents, the Frosts, lived only two blocks away. "Grandpa Frost had a cow named May," said Bruce. "When I was just seven years of age, Grandpa taught me how to milk her. She was a beautiful, light chestnut-coloured Holstein. May was gentle of nature and easy to milk, even for a little boy with small hands."

Every time Bruce entered his grandfather's tiny, four-stall barn, he was told to be careful when walking behind the cow. "'As soon as the cow lifts her tail, clear out,' Grandpa stressed. 'A tail in the air only means one thing!' And I knew exactly what that was."

One beautiful, warm, summer day, Bruce decided to visit his grandparents down the street. His grandmother was working in the garden not far from the barn, and Bruce asked for permission to milk the cow. "Grandma walked me to the barn, making sure I had a milking stool and a clean bucket. She also informed me that May had been eating greens, which had given her diarrhea. "'Be sure not to stand behind May,' she cautioned. I promised to be careful, and as Grandma returned to her vegetable patch, I settled into milking the cow. Feeling very grown up, I chatted to May as she continued to chew her cud and I slowly filled my bucket.

"Suddenly, the barn door burst open and Grandpa stood silhouetted against the sunlight. 'Hey, what are you doing in here?' he called out. 'I'm milking May,' I replied.

"'You're getting pretty good at that,' he said. Then, just as Grandpa turned to walk to the other end of the barn, May's tail rose straight towards the ceiling. 'Grandpa, look out!' I hollered. Grandpa was frozen in place as a lightening-fast stream of liquid covered him from head to toe in a viscous, green mixture of chewed veggies and brown water. Encased in a smelly, gooey mess, Grandpa opened first one eye then the other. I was speechless, not believing what I was seeing. Words came out of my grandpa's mouth that my seven-year-old ears had never heard before. Many of the words I didn't know the meaning of, but it was clear to me that Grandpa was not happy.

"Attracted by all that ruckus, Grandma hurried towards us. As she came closer, taking a good look at Grandpa, she started to laugh uncontrollably. She made it to the garden hose at the back of the house and told Grandpa, 'Willy, stand still!' Laughing hysterically, she sprayed him off. About halfway through the rinse cycle, Grandpa started laughing, too. It was then that I realized I was not in trouble," said Bruce.

"After Grandpa had gone to the house for a long, hot bath, I called out for Grandma to come to the barn. There on the wall, directly behind May, was a perfect outline of Grandpa. I remember clean cement surrounded by a nicely textured, remarkably smelly, green mixture. Conspiratorially, Grandma leaned over and whispered, 'Don't wash that off just yet.' Over the next half hour, Grandma enjoyed herself tremendously, arranging tours for family, friends, and neighbours.

"Many tears of laughter were shed over the next couple of days, until Grandpa asked me to hose the wall off. There must be some powerful ingredient in cow poop, because a faint outline of grandpa was visible on that wall for a very long time," Bruce laughed.

Memories from the Best of Buds

Rose, Anne, Beth, and LaVerne were a tight-knit group of friends growing up together in Lucan. Rose Revington was born in 1939, LaVerne George in 1940, Beth Watson and Rose's sister, Anne, in 1941. LaVerne was the only one of the original foursome not from the area. She was born in one of my favourite provinces, Prince Edward Island. When she was six, her father, Dr. Clayton George, a family physician, came to set up his practice in the village.

LaVerne never felt like an outsider because Beth, the daughter of the local dentist, Dr. Thomas Watson, became her instant friend. Beth introduced LaVerne to her other friends, Rose and Anne. They were the daughters of Wesley Revington, a beef farmer and owner of Revington's Meat Market. "We became the best of buds!" LaVerne told me as we sat in the living room of her London home.

"When we were between eight and ten years of age," LaVerne recalled, "our mothers introduced us to figure skating. As Lucan didn't have an arena, we were forced to go to London. In front of Lucan's Central Hotel, with great anticipation we would board a huge, red and white Motorways bus that would carry our figure skates and us safely to the big city. We felt so grown up, travelling on our own." Beth was quick to point out: "Looking at it from today's perspective, it was quite a daring adventure. As soon as the driver dropped us off at the bus terminal, we had to find the London Arena without much help from anyone. Can you imagine parents in today's world letting their young children go without a chaperon?"

As much as the girls treasured their excursions into London, it all came to an end when the Lucan Community Memorial Centre was completed in 1950. LaVerne's mother, Elsie, was instrumental in finding an instructor willing to teach in Lucan. It wasn't long before the Lucan Figure Skating Club was formed. "My friend Marg Neil," said LaVerne, "was the best figure skater of all the girls in the area. The skating club was lots of fun and we were especially proud of our annual ice carnival. Of course, Rose and I were always partners."

"As we got older, figure skating was no longer the cool thing to do," smiled Beth.

"However," LaVerne added, "we didn't give up skating altogether. There was public skating on Saturdays and Sundays, which became very important to us. The reason for our newfound interest was boys, of course. We skated together with the boys and even held hands. Unless we were stricken by a severe illness, no weekend was ever missed. We had lots of fun during those long winter months."

And what was there to do in the summer? Did the "best of buds" swim in Lucan's two

The Best of Buds: Rose and Anne Revington, LaVerne George, and Beth Watson

famous swimming holes, Rock Bottom or Seales? I personally have fond memories of frequenting both places after school with my friends, jumping into the cool, dark water in our birthday suits.

LaVerne looked at me in horror: "Those were two of the most horrible places that I knew of in the world. To get a bloodsucker stuck between my toes . . . or to run into those silly boys . . . I don't think so! Coming from the East Coast, I was used to swimming in the clear blue ocean every summer; those awful mudholes just could not compete."

Beth clearly remembers one eventful morning on March 12th, 1953. She was still asleep as her mother burst into her room urging her to look out of her bedroom window. Peering through the glass, Beth could see the Lucan Public School, directly across the street, engulfed in flames. "I couldn't believe what I was seeing," she recalls. "As I watched in horror, the school burned to the ground. Apparently, overheated pipes caused the blaze."

Over the next twelve months, the entire student body took all their classes in church halls and at the arena while a new school was being constructed. This turned out to be quite an adventure for most of us. In March of 1954, exactly a year later, the new public school opened. Rose, Beth, and LaVerne became the first class to attend Grade 8 in the new building. Shortly after moving into the new school, an event of much discussion occurred. "A local girl not much older than we were got married. This created much excitement," Beth recalled. "We all took the afternoon off school to watch the wedding. On the lawn of the Anglican Church

we stood in awe, gawking at this child bride. Looking back, I realize we didn't even have permission to leave the school that afternoon." With a wide smile, Beth said, "I guess we were playing hooky! We were all still so innocent then."

"At that time of our lives, we all became very interested in music, especially as the Lucan Arena hosted such well-known entertainers as Johnny Cash, the Everly Brothers, and Marty Robbins," LaVerne said. "Another area event we attended faithfully was the Lucan Irish Six hockey games. We made a point of always arriving early at the arena to secure the best seats. We just loved to watch those young men play. My father was the team doctor, a position he enjoyed tremendously. There were a number of occasions when players would come back to our house for a steak dinner after the game. I don't know how my mother put up with having to supply food to a team of hungry hockey players, but I was certainly thrilled and the envy of my girlfriends."

Beth (Watson) Radcliffe and LaVerne (George) Revington went on to become public school teachers, marry, and have children. Anne (Revington) Wilson had a thirty-eight-year career with London Transit, buying buses in the purchasing department. She married and had two sons. Rose (Revington) Lawrence became a dental assistant for her brother, Dr. Harvey Revington, in his London practice. Shortly after her marriage, Rose incurred serious injuries in a severe automobile accident. Sadly, she died on the 17th of September 1999.

Canada's First Woman School Bus Driver

The London Free Press regional correspondent Jennie Raycraft Lewis wrote in an early 1950s article: "Betty Drennan is a trailblazer for being the first-ever woman school bus driver."

On the 6th of September 1960, I photographed Betty behind the wheel of her large, yellow school bus. This photograph accompanied an article in both *The London Free Press* and the *Exeter Times Advocate*, marking the occasion of Betty's thirteenth year of driving students to school.

How did this woman, born in 1920 on a London Township farm, get to be a trailblazer? "I came to driving school buses in a roundabout way," Betty said, smiling. "It was the spring of 1947, and Dad, a farmer foremost and a school bus driver secondarily, was busy planting his crops. He was working every possible daylight hour and needed someone to drive the school bus for him the following day. When he asked me, I jumped at the chance, even though I'd never driven a bus before. In those days, a special licence was not required, and I found driving the old bus with fourteen children aboard a breeze and lots of fun. It was an old clunker," she said

with a chuckle. "It was big and hard to steer, but I always made it around the corners."

When Medway High School in Arva opened that same fall, Lucan High School became Lucan Public School. Betty, who was now driving full time, was assigned a new, larger bus. Her route expanded and she had to transport forty to forty-five students. "Compared to my old bus, this was like driving a Cadillac," she laughed. "Being on time got a little more complex with that many passengers to coordinate. It was very important to me to pick up each student at his or her farm gate at the same time each day. This wasn't always easy to do. We had some pretty rough winters back then. The Mooresville Road was always a ripper! After a snowstorm, Tom Hodgins, the road superintendent for Biddulph Township, made sure a snowplow went out ahead of us, clearing the road and keeping us safe. The sun could be shining on the high school grounds in Arva, but here in the north country it would be snowing and drifting. The weather was often very unpredictable.

"I never forget the afternoon of March 6th, 1963. I was driving the students home and the snowdrifts were at least four feet high on the

In 1960 Betty Drennan began her 13th year of school bus driving. This photograph, taken by the author, appeared in the *London Free Press* and the *Exeter Times Advocate*.

Marguerite McRoberts took up the account: "I opened the door to find three young girls wanting to use our bathroom. After they explained their situation, I suggested they bring the rest of the students to our home to get warm. Fortunately the telephone was working, and we contacted all of the parents and also called the township snowplow. By the time everyone had arrived at the farm, it was almost suppertime and we had fifty-two hungry teens on our hands. Our roast beef supper did not quite stretch that far, so we raided the pantry. The kids made short work of all the bread, crackers, and cans of salmon, as well as cookies and muffins. I have to say that we were all very impressed with the good manners and polite behaviour of these teens."

About eight-thirty in the evening the McRobertses received a call informing them that a bus would pick the students up at Highway 7, about half a mile away. Some of the students walked while others took a ride in the small trailer behind Ross's tractor. Betty added: "I felt sorry for

Coursey Line. The wind was whipping across a cut and I could not see a thing because of continuous whiteouts. It wasn't long before I got stuck. Three of my students braved the storm and went for help to a neighbouring farmhouse owned by Marguerite and Ross McRoberts."

Marguerite. When we eventually left, her floors were soaked with melted snow and her cupboards were bare."

A couple of days later, to Marguerite's great surprise, the school bus once more stopped at the farm gate. "A couple of students came to the door handing me a 'thank you' card and money they had collected on the bus so that I could stock up my pantry again. It's good to be prepared," Marguerite laughed. "It was an unforgettable experience for all of us."

I asked Betty if she had ever encountered trouble on the bus. "Well, for the most part, they were pretty good kids," she recalled. "However, there was one afternoon I observed two boys fighting, and it looked pretty serious. I stopped the bus, walked back, and sternly told the two to stop. One of them, Don Coughlin, stopped immediately, but the other boy continued to take shots at him, punching him on the head. I felt so bad for Don. Listening to me got him a smashed face.

"On another occasion, three boys were giving me a hard time. We were close to Lucan when I pulled the bus over, turned around, and told them to stop or get off. They stopped, but as soon as my back was turned, they started up again. Stopping the bus a second time, I ordered them off. Protesting, they stepped down onto the road and began their mile-long walk to the village. I was no sooner home when one of the mothers called me on the phone, berating me. How could I make her boy walk in the cold without his winter boots? I explained the situation to her, but she insisted that her son was innocent and I was wrong. That was the roughest time I ever had. None of the other parents called

to complain. The irate mother was fairly new to Lucan. I guess she didn't really know me."

At Christmas and at the end of each school year, Betty always received a special gift from the students on her bus. They would take up a collection and purchase a present for her. "Each gift was very thoughtful. I've got some great old memories of those days," said Betty.

In 1972, Betty had a heart attack. It was seven o'clock in the morning and she was still in bed. Betty was only fifty-two years of age and just beginning her twenty-fifth year of driving. At the end of her convalescence, Michael Murphy, the bus line owner, asked her to return to work. Betty declined. "I was worried about having a heart attack while driving a school bus. I felt it was too risky and didn't want to put anyone in harm's way."

Betty was paid $4.00 a day when she started driving in 1947. At the end of her career in 1972, she made $22.00 a day. Over her entire twenty-four-year career driving a school bus, Betty never had an accident. "I am proud of that, of course. But mostly, it was just a wonderful experience. I never thought about being a trailblazer."

Unfortunately, Betty Drennan passed away on September 13th, 2003. Her four children, nine grandchildren, and four great-grandchildren greatly miss her.

I feel privileged to have had the opportunity to talk and laugh with Betty towards the end of her life.

Things are not what they seem

I remember walking through the door of Lucan Public School on Market Street with my cousin Wayne Culbert, both of us eager to start our first day in Grade 1. Miss Taylor, our teacher, assigned me a seat right next to Joe Hodgins. I instantly took a liking to Joe, a farm boy from Saintsbury Line. We both felt a little apprehensive, not quite sure what was expected of us. Our uneasiness was soon forgotten as we watched cousin Wayne make his way to the back of the room to sharpen his pencil. Not satisfied with the task itself, Wayne proceeded with great concentration to dismantle the sharpener housing. Small metal parts were neatly and carefully placed on the windowsill. Joe and I collapsed in laughter as Miss Taylor chastised inquisitive cousin Wayne.

Of course, it was not all fun and laughter. I struggled with arithmetic while Joe struggled with reading. I never knew the severity of Joe's reading problem, and the origin of that problem was never diagnosed by anyone. This was the late forties, and no one had ever heard of dyslexia. Joe recalls: "As far back as I can remember, I had problems reading. All the letters were backwards and the great frustration was that neither my teachers nor my parents had a clue what was going on. Any time I attempted to read, I would get very frustrated, while my teacher would rap my knuckles with a yardstick, accusing me of not paying attention. There was no diagnosis of my reading disability, no remedial help, and no understanding."

Dyslexia affects all kinds of people regardless of intelligence, race, or social background. Today, thankfully, there are many resources available and the effects of dyslexia can largely be overcome by skilled specialist teachings. For Joe there was nothing available at all. As the years passed, the teachers would simply push him through the system until, at the age of sixteen in Grade 7, he was legally able to leave school, which he did.

Growing up in Lucan, Joe and I spent quite a bit of time with each other. I loved playing with his Meccano set, the first one in the village. Joe had a knack of building intricate structures. However, Joe's favourite object was a small telescope he received at the age of ten. The night skies held great fascination for Joe, and for a number of years he travelled into London with a family friend from Clandeboye to attend monthly observatory meetings. Joe was thrilled to be allowed to look through the giant telescope at the University of Western Ontario's observatory. By his early twenties, Joe had joined the Royal Astronomical Society of Canada.

For many years, Joe worked part time as a maintenance man at Lucan Lanes, the local bowling alley. The owner was very pleased with Joe's work ethic and planned to send him to the Brunswick Manufacturing School on a technical course. Joe had to decline because of his reading disability. Once more he was penalized for something beyond his control. At the age of twenty-one, Joe began working full time for Selby Shoes in London, putting steel shanks and heels on footwear. When the Selby plant closed for good, Joe was hired by Kaschper Racing Shells just down the road from his family farm.

During his twenty-three years at the boat works, he had the opportunity to work at a lot of different jobs.

Today, Joe is retired and dedicates most of his time to his love of digital photography. Nature is his favourite subject, especially birds that he captures on both his video and digital still cameras. When asked how his life might have been different had he been diagnosed early on in his childhood, he pondered the possibilities: "I would have loved a career in communications and satellites. That's the stuff I've really gotten into and that's what holds my interest. Things are not always what they seem. If I would not have been labelled by the system as a slow learner and if I could have received proper help, my education would have been more substantial and my life certainly would have taken a different path."

Joe Hodgins's passions are outer space and nature photography.

Honorary Five-Star General

When the American Legion learned of Lucan's Bill Smith and his contributions to their military veterans' seniors' programs, they bestowed upon him the title of Honorary Five-Star General. The event took the form of a tribute dinner held in Niagara Falls, New York, in 1987. In December of 2002, Bill Smith was recognized again, this time in Canada, for his volunteer work. The Commemorative Medal from Her Majesty Queen Elizabeth II's Golden Jubilee is awarded to individuals who have made significant contributions to Canada, to their community, or to their fellow Canadians. Bill Smith was at the top of the list in all three categories.

I've known Bill since my childhood. As a boy, I delivered the *Toronto Star* to his home every day. On my way to this interview, I was flooded with memories as I approached his Beech Street home. I realized that I was walking along the path I had walked four and a half decades earlier, delivering his papers.

James William Smith was born in 1920. As a teenager living in Grand Valley, near Orangeville, Ontario, he decided to join the Royal Canadian Navy. In 1944, he met and fell in love with Lorraine King, whom he married shortly thereafter. They both returned to Halifax, where Bill was stationed. After his 1945 discharge, the couple moved to Ontario and settled in the small village of Erin, north of Guelph.

Bill had always been mindful of others less fortunate than himself. It was not long before the ex-serviceman saw a need to help his fellow veterans and their families. He did so by assisting with paperwork, obtaining military pensions from the Canadian government, and helping widows of servicemen killed in action. In 1946, he was instrumental in establishing Erin's Royal Canadian Legion Hall.

At the same time, Bill's and Lorraine's infant son Bryan was dying of an undetermined illness that baffled their doctor and left the family without hope. A friend of Bill's late father, Colonel Fitzgerald, referred the couple to Dr. Goodfellow in London, Ontario, who finally diagnosed Bryan with celiac disease, a rare intestinal disorder of young children. "Thanks to Colonel Fitzgerald and Dr. Goodfellow, our son was saved," said Bill.

In 1950, the Smith family, which now included daughter Maureen, moved to Lucan, where Bill used his skills to establish the Lucan Legion Hall. Bill rose through the ranks to become zone commander, district commander, and provincial president for Ontario, Dominion Command vice-president, and National Poppy Chairman. "I was involved with Veterans Services, presenting briefs to parliamentary

When the Queen Mother visited Parkwood Hospital in London, Ontario, Bill Smith was there to greet her. He is pictured on the right. The Honorary Five-Star General stands next to the veterans' monument in front of the Lucan Legion.

committees. For example, there were no geriatric chairs in Canada, and the Legion started sponsoring three doctors a year on a national level." After the program became a success in Canada, the American Legion invited Bill to the United States to share his expertise. He became involved in a number of their programs and so impressed his neighbours to the south that they presented him with the Honorary Five-Star General Award.

Bill's outstanding record with Veterans Services led to an invitation to Buckingham Palace in London, England. "One of the highlights of my life was that invitation to the Canada Day celebration at Buckingham Palace. Any function taking place at the palace has to be rehearsed. Arriving the day prior to the big event, we were met by the head of the palace guard. He took us through the routine, familiarizing us with proper protocol. Most important was the Guardsman Salute. This was not an easy feat. I worried endlessly about tripping and disgracing myself before the Queen Mom. The following day at Buckingham Palace, I was overcome by nerves, forgetting everything I had been taught, and promptly executed my Navy Salute in front of the Queen Mother. To my utter amazement, Her Majesty winked at me. At the end of the ceremony, I was still in a daze as Her Majesty, accompanied by her aide, approached me and said: "We spotted navy!" She took my hand and told me all about her parents. Her father was navy, and her brother and husband were navy as well. So steeped in navy was the Queen Mother that she didn't have ladies-in-waiting, only gentlemen-in-waiting who were all retired admirals."

That encounter became Bill's much-loved event, until two years later when the Queen Mother came to visit Canada. She was scheduled to see Parkwood Hospital in London, Ontario, and Bill was given the honour of greeting Her Majesty. "I watched her step out of the official vehicle, and as she approached, I saluted. She smiled, winked, took my hand and said to me, 'So happy to see you again!' I was dumbfounded. How could she have remembered me? As she continued her walkabout, her secretary explained: 'As soon as she saw you, she recognized you.' The Queen Mother, then in her nineties, still possessed a sharp mind. What a grand person and what a wonderful lady! I will never forget that day and will cherish the experience forever."

On the second of May 2005, I telephoned Bill at his home in Lucan. I literally caught him as he was going out the door to catch a plane for France. Bill and his daughter, Maureen Smith, a French professor at London's University of Western Ontario, and her children Paul and Catherine, were going to a memorial and commemorative service for six Canadian airmen, one of them Bill's friend Wilfred Gordon Harris of Grand Valley, Ontario. On the 23rd of May 1944, Sgt. Harris and his five colleagues died when their Whitley bomber was blown out of the sky by German anti-aircraft guns. That fateful evening, the Canadians were dropping information pamphlets to the residents of Sèes a few hundred feet below. The Royal Canadian Air Force was telling the French community that help was near, that they should not give up hope.

The crash was devastating. The plane and crew were burned beyond recognition. The charred remains were buried in a mass grave with burial records identifying them as "*aviateurs inconnus*" (unknown aviators). For the past sixty years, the only information the airmen's families in Canada had was "missing in action."

Roger Cornevan was a young boy when he witnessed the bomber plummet to the earth in a ball of fire. In 1998, after retirement, he returned to his hometown of Sèes, determined to uncover the wartime mystery. Following a lot of uncanny sleuthing, the names of the six crewmembers were finally uncovered. After sixty years, there are now answers for the family and friends of the six brave airmen. The French erected a granite monument at the crash site to honour their fallen allies.

Bill Smith went to France to pay respects to his "Grand Valley" friend Sgt. Harris. One of Bill's fellow travellers was Ralph Woods, another friend of the Harris family. Ralph and Bill had not seen one another for more than six decades. Coincidentally, I've known Bill Smith since childhood, and Ralph Woods is one of my neighbours on Amherst Island, where we both now reside.

Bill returned from his trip to France feeling privileged to have been part of that commemorative service. More than ever, at the age of eighty-five, he is fully committed to helping and honouring his fellow servicemen and servicewomen.

Ralph Woods of Amherst Island photographed Bill Smith in France at the site where six Canadian airmen died. Ralph and Bill were close friends of Sgt. Wilfred Gordon Harris of Grand Valley, Ontario, pictured in his Royal Canadian Air Force uniform.

Hammer, Saw, and a Set of Clubs

Thomas Arthur Weller has been my good friend since the age of ten. Living above my parents' store, I could see Tom's house from my bedroom window. I often observed Tom's father leaving the house very early in the morning to drive his fruit and vegetable transport for Sansone Fruit Company of London. Tom's mother was one of the finest bakers and candy makers in Lucan.

At an early age, it was obvious that Tom was gifted with a hammer and saw. Like most boys, we loved playing cowboys. With only a scrap of lumber at hand, Tom skillfully cut out the shape of two US Cavalry rifles. As the budding artist, I was responsible for giving them colour and design. We spent hours playing in the countryside, never tiring of our make-believe games.

When Tom and I graduated from Lucan Public School, we both followed our dreams. In London, I studied commercial art at Beal Tech, and Tom majored in construction at Clark Road High School. After completing our secondary education, we both became apprentices. Tom became a carpenter for Ellis-Don Construction, and I began a forty-two-year career in television news starting at CFPL TV.

We rented an apartment together located in an old, well-maintained brick building, which was later torn down to make way for the London City Hall—we have the dubious fame to have lived where the London City Hall now stands. The first home away from home was a great experience for two eighteen-year-olds. We discovered all of the interesting things in life that most young men hope to discover.

After a couple of years of bachelor life, Tom moved on. By then he had met and married a beautiful young woman from Holland named Dorothy Rynen. Tom's career with Ellis-Don was taking him to construction projects from Nova Scotia to Alberta. "I'm one of the few Canadian construction workers who can say they've built a stadium," said Tom. The project he was referring to is the Commonwealth Game Stadium in Edmonton, which was contracted to Ellis-Don to be completed for the 1978 games.

Although Tom had achieved many of his goals, after eighteen years of working for London-based Ellis-Don, he became restless. His wife and children were tired of moving around the country, uprooting their home every few years. Tom made the decision to resign in 1979, as did two of his co-workers. Together with a London concrete supplier they decided to form their own company and named it Tonda Construction. By 1989, Tom's partners had either retired or had been bought out, leaving Tom as the sole owner. At the time, Tonda was generating $2.5 million dollars in business. A year later, Tom had more than doubled his

Sitting on the author's 1961 Austin Healey Sprite, twenty-year-old Tom Weller strums a Beatles tune.

contracts to seven million dollars. "I can happily say that by the end of 2004, Tonda Construction had acquired contracts worth over thirty-five million dollars. Our bread-and-butter jobs are with the University of Western Ontario and the London Health Science Centre. The largest project we've worked on to date was a seventeen million-dollar contract, building the London Central Library. When we completed the job, we donated twenty-five thousand dollars to the Library. They named one of their meeting rooms in our honour. When we hear a radio announcer speak of a meeting in the Central Library's Tonda Room, it feels good that we were able to give back to the community," Tom said proudly.

Tom's daughter Tracey was the first family member to join the firm. She became treasurer and office manager. When son Darrin came aboard, he was immediately sent into the field. Tom wanted him to start in the trenches to gain valuable experience, as Tom had done himself. In the mid-'90s, Darrin became a project manager and today he is the vice-president of Tonda Construction. "My wife, Dorothy, was the last to join the team and is now in charge of human resources."

Tom has always known the importance of taking time out from his busy schedule. One of his favourite pastimes is golf. He has played the sport since his mid-twenties. "I loved playing a course called Fairvilla located near Nilestown. The course was later renamed Willow Park, and I had a dream of someday owning it. That dream became reality twenty years later when I had the opportunity to purchase the course. I renamed it The Willows Golf and Country Club, a name more befitting its function."

Just north of Highway 401, nestled alongside Highway 74, The Willows Golf and Country Club is a par-68 course measuring 5,375 yards. Guarded by a creek across the front of the green, *London Free Press* golf reporter John Herbert calls the 192-yard sixth, the "best hole." Tom has constructed a driving range and a new clubhouse with a large outside deck overlooking the eighteenth green. Thirty new power golf carts replaced the ten worn originals. Daughter Tracey, when not wearing her Tonda Construction hat, is responsible for the day-to-day operation of the golf course. "It's my baby," Tom said. "We've turned it into one of the nicest little golf courses in the London area. I don't plan to retire in the near future. When I eventually leave construction, I plan to buzz around the course on a sit-down lawn tractor in the mornings and play golf all afternoon. Wouldn't that be the ideal retirement?"

In the meantime, Tom relaxes at home listening to his favourite music by Elvis Presley. He started collecting seventy-eights when we were boys growing up in Lucan. Today he has in his library of vinyls, tapes, and CDs everything that Elvis ever produced. "I'll never forget the day Elvis died. It was like the day John F. Kennedy was shot. I went into mourning for a few days," Tom recalled.

"He went into mourning for a whole week!" laughed Dorothy.

Tom has not only followed his dream but also has succeeded far beyond his wildest boyhood imagination.

Scuba Diving Hairstylist

Halfway through coiffing a client's hair in her London salon, Marlyn (Fevery) Smith, born and raised in the Lucan area, received an unusual phone call. The male voice at the other end asked if she had ever participated in a Lake Ontario dive.

Yes, she had! "Could you tell me something about the depth and what the bottom is like?" asked the man. Marlyn's curiosity was piqued: "Did you lose something off your boat—do you need help retrieving it?" she queried.

"I've been searching for someone with technical diving skills," the man replied, "and everyone I have been in contact with mentions your name, suggesting that you can help me with a project I'm working on. I am looking for the nine missing test models of the Avro Arrow. I've got all the coordinates and I need you to lead the dive team," he explained.

The caller's name was Bill Scott, a former Canadian Air Force engineer. He was passionate about his project: "It seems a shame and a waste for a significant part of Canadian history to be just lying at the bottom of Lake Ontario. Canadians deserve to have those pieces of history displayed in their museums."

The models, with wingspans of nearly two metres (six feet, three inches) and weighing roughly 217 kg (478 pounds) each, were built to test the stability of the CF–105 Avro Arrow design and to determine the possibility of supersonic flight. The models were fired from rockets over Lake Ontario near Point Petre in Prince Edward County from 1954 to 1956.

The CF–105 Avro Arrow was a revolutionary jet interceptor, designed and built by the A.V. Roe Aircraft Company of Canada. On the 4th of October 1957, the same day the USSR launched the Sputnik satellite, the Arrow was rolled out onto the tarmac. It was to be North America's first line of defence against the supersonic bombers believed to be under construction in the Soviet Union. It was designed to intercept Soviet bombers over the Arctic during the Cold War era.

On February 20th, 1959, the Arrow project was cancelled, and 14,000 workers lost their jobs; that day became known as "Black Friday." The late Prime Minister John Diefenbaker's government scuttled the project. Canada's aerospace industry was crippled by the controversial decision, ending before it really began.

Marlyn knew about the Avro Arrow project and was instantly intrigued and excited about Bill Scott's request and mission. The project required experienced divers able to plunge forty-five to sixty metres below the surface of Lake Ontario, much deeper than recreational dives. The special equipment used includes a side-scan,

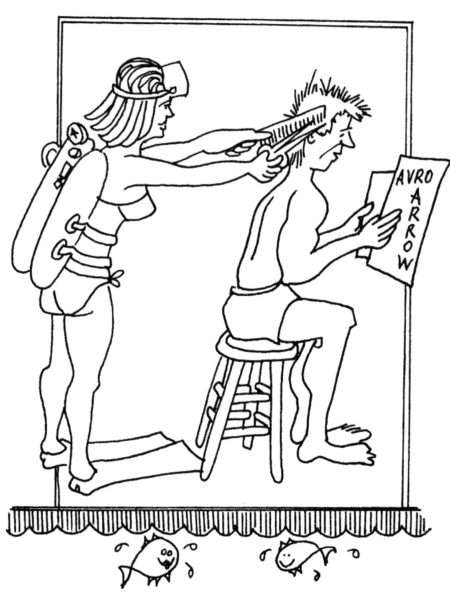

which is a torpedo-shaped device that is pulled through the water picking up ultra-sounds off the lake bottom. The dive team would depend on the research supplied by Scott and his volunteers. Scott claimed to be able to pinpoint within 2,000 metres the location of three of the Avro models. "I never expected to stumble onto anything this big," said Marlyn, who is not only a hairdresser, but is also a professional scuba diving instructor. She has been diving for over nineteen years and is involved in many of Ontario's diving activities.

Marlyn is now the vice-president of the non-profit group Arrow Recovery Canada. She carries all dive responsibilities for the recovery team. Marlyn is also the founder of GLID, Great Lakes In Depth, formed to keep up an interest of diving in our Great Lakes.

Where is the Avro Arrow test model recovery project today? The first dive took place in August of 1998 and the project is still ongoing. The team was able to make contact with Carmon Johnson, the last person still alive who witnessed the Avro model firings. With Carmon's help, they were able to confirm all of the bearings. Despite this information and intensive searching, the dive team has been unable to locate the Avro models so far. However, they did discover a schooner wreck believed to be the *Persia* that sank in September 1894. She was a stone carrier on her way from Kingston to Toronto. En route, with a cargo of heavy stone, she opened up and went down off Point Petre. Her crew escaped in the yawl boat along with their pet raccoon, which had sailed aboard the *Persia* for many seasons.

Marlyn Smith has always loved water, and even as a small child never feared the wet element. "As long as I can remember, water always fascinated me. I loved watching underwater shows, especially the Jacque Cousteau documentaries. My dream was to be part of a dive some time in my life!" she said. Very athletic, Marlyn played softball for fifteen years with the Lucan Spitfires, but it was on a trip to Cuba with friends that she fell in love with the underwater world. "I basically spent two weeks snorkelling, with my face in the water, returning to Canada with a tanned back and a pale face," she recalls. Within two years of her Cuban experience, she had received her master's level in scuba diving and became a dive master. "I was so into it, it took over my life . . . it consumed me!" she said.

Today, her adult daughters Amanda and Loren, both of Lucan, are certified divers, and, like their mom, they are both avid ball players. Living north of London, Marlyn has her own hair salon operating out of her home, and, most importantly, she owns a specially designed swimming pool where she teaches scuba diving.

"Dive with Mar" is a scuba diving educational facility that offers customized courses and charters from basic dives to mixed gas technical training, including instructor certificate training at all levels.

Known to her friends as "Mar," she is a cave-diving enthusiast and one of the best all-round divers and instructors. Her students come from all walks of life. Her most unusual request came from a sixty-seven-year-old woman who wanted to take lessons but worried that she might be too old for the sport. Marlyn put her at ease: "If you have the drive to do it, I have the patience to teach you. We'll take it slow, do it at your own pace." The woman took the lessons required, loving every moment. "You are never too old to take up scuba diving," laughed Marlyn.

In May of each year, the dive team gets ready to start their search. "I'm always looking forward to a new season, but it's like looking for a needle in a haystack," claims Marlyn. "The search is part of the challenge. It has been a tremendous experience. We are strictly volunteers, all people who believe in this project!"

Marlyn maintains there is no greater adventure than scuba diving. The excitement of discovery and exploration of the underwater world is something she plans to immerse herself in for many years to come.

Visit her Web site:
www.divewithmar.on.ca

Oceanic 46

In 1980, Gary and Jackie King bought a home on Saintsbury Line near Lucan, with enough acreage to build a barn-style workshop. The Kings' dream of single-handedly constructing an ocean-going sailboat would finally become reality.

Five years later, Jackie, a nurse at London's University Hospital, and Gary, who at the time was a technical advisor at 3M, pulled out their blueprints and began construction of their

Jackie and Gary King are single-handedly constructing their dream ocean-going sailboat. They hope to complete the Oceanic 46 by the spring of 2006.

Custom Oceanic 46 sailboat. "This is our hobby," Jackie explained. "People often ask why it takes so long to build a boat. None of the parts come from your local building centre. Everything has to be handmade, every corner, every piece of furniture, every cupboard, it all is custom made. Each piece is painstakingly crafted by Gary, and that's why it takes so long."

The Kings are hoping to complete their boat by the spring of 2006 and launch it in Goderich harbour. Their Lucan property will be sold shortly after the launch, making the sailboat their primary home. They will spend the summer sailing Georgian Bay and the North Channel of Manitoulin Island, one of their favourite areas. Sometime in the fall, they'll head south to the Caribbean in search of warmer climes. "It's going to be a long, leisurely cruise of up to ten years. There are a lot of places we want to see around the world. We can sail into any port, leave the boat anchored, and go on shore trips, exploring the country and getting to know the people who live there," she said. "We are planning to spend a couple of years in the Caribbean, living off the boat and backpacking. We will travel through Panama into the South Pacific; spend at least another two years in New Zealand and Australia, and then on to the Mediterranean. Ten years might not be enough," Jackie laughed.

Gary has been working on his "retirement hobby" for over twenty years now and is thrilled that the project has almost come to completion. The boat design is based on a stock plan created by Ted Brewer, who has designed over 260 boats. Brewer, originally from Hamilton, Ontario, made his professional career in the United States and now lives on Gabriola Island in British Columbia. Any boat designed by Ted Brewer holds instant respect.

Gary explained: "This design is a 46-foot pilot house flush-deck sailboat. We made a couple of modifications to suit our purpose. After completion, the boat will weigh 38,000 to 40,000 pounds. When cruising the world, you require a moderate displacement boat for good ocean sailing. Our boat is forty-six feet in length and thirteen and one-half feet wide. It is basically being set up for the two of us. Our main sleeping cabin is the aft cabin. The forward cabin is for guests. We can comfortably sleep six people, but in a pinch can accommodate eight. At times, on long stretches of ocean sailing, we may bring extra crew members on board. Hopefully some of our friends will be available and up to the task.

"The boat itself is designed with an inside steering station, so in heavier weather, we can go down below and close everything off. The boat can basically be managed from inside the cabin. We fully expect at some time in our voyage that we'll probably roll. The windows in the pilothouse have heavy storm boards that bolt over top of it. In case of horrendous weather, we can cover everything, go below, and be well protected from the elements. As much as you try to avoid heavy weather, once out on the ocean you sometimes get caught.

"On a large boat like the Oceanic 46, there is a lot of space," continued Gary. "If one of us needs some private time, there are many different areas for solitary pursuits. We can go forward to the salon, which has comfortable seating to read or watch TV, or one of us can be in the pilot house or the aft cabin."

The ship has two heads (toilets) complete with a shower in each. The well-laid-out galley (kitchen) has a fairly large fridge and freezer system, big enough to stock meat for a year. The boat is set up to be almost entirely self-sufficient. The Kings will make their own drinking water from the sea. There's a generator on board that can power all the systems, including the air conditioner and a good computer. They carry enough fuel to cover 1,800 miles under power.

"The mast is made out of aluminum," Gary said. "Everything needs to be convenient, because at our age, it is almost like geriatric sailing. The sails will all be furling, which means they wrap themselves up to store with the help of power winches. The boat has been set up for the two of us to operate; all winches are powered, there's very little heavy, manual work to be done. The anchor windlass is powered and there's a bow thruster to help us manoeuvre when docking. Mind you, we don't plan to do a lot of docking. We prefer to be at anchor somewhere and go to shore in our dinghy. We actually have two dinghies and a full enclosure life raft."

Gary and Jackie are both experienced sailors. They have owned boats throughout their lives, at least three prior to the Oceanic 46. The last boat they owned was a thirty-two-foot

Bayfield, built in the Lake Huron village of Bayfield, Ontario. They refurbished it and sailed it for a few years. One day, an American spotted the boat, fell in love with it, made an offer, and the Bayfield was sold. That was the point in time when the Kings decided to focus more effort on building their own vessel and shortly thereafter what was an evening work project became a full-time plan. Why is it important to Gary to construct his own sailboat? "Most people think it is more economical, but frankly, that is a fallacy," explained Gary. "For me, it is all about the challenge, the problem-solving, knowing that it is our own creation."

Franklin Roosevelt said: "Happiness lies in the joy of achievement and the thrill of creative effort." Gary and Jackie have been actively involved in the process of creating their dream for the past two decades, inspired by the prospect of visiting distant shores and cultures. They aptly named their boat *Inspiration Lady*.

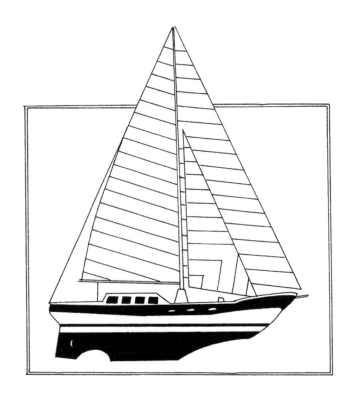

The Official Tooth Puller
of Lucan Public School

The official tooth puller of Lucan Public School is not a dentist, but a teacher. Marguerite McRoberts taught Grades 2, 3, and 4 at Lucan Public School. "After the birth of my daughters Tami and Terri, I retired for seven years," she explained, "but returned to teaching in September of 1971.

"I took over the Grade 1 class vacated by Muriel Cobleigh. Muriel had reigned supreme for over twenty years, and those were big shoes to fill. She was well loved and very competent," Marguerite said. "At Muriel's retirement party, she presented me with a pair of dentist's pliers. I was quite bewildered. Muriel explained to me that they were used for extracting teeth. The late Lucan dentist, Doctor Tom Watson, had given them to her with instructions on how to pull teeth, which were now generously forwarded on to me. I felt a little apprehensive, especially at first.

"As everyone knows, six-year-olds are prime candidates for loose baby teeth. I was called upon many times during my sixteen years of teaching Grade 1, and became known as the school's official tooth puller! Parents have told me that their children refused to allow them to pull a tooth," she laughed. "Part of that was probably the fact that I entered the tooth owner's name into the tooth fairy book, exhibited in the classroom. The children also received an official-looking piece of paper displaying their taped-on tooth. The boys and girls then left the paper under their pillow, proof for the tooth fairy to do her job.

"Years later, Mary Holden, one of my former students, told me that she had saved a note written by me addressed to the tooth fairy. Apparently, after I pulled out Mary's tooth, it went missing. Quick to remedy the dilemma, I penned a note to the tooth fairy asking her to please give Mary her well-deserved monetary reward."

It was not uncommon to have children lining up at recess outside Marguerite McRoberts's classroom door waiting their turn to see the official tooth puller. When asked if she has had any mishaps, she replied: "Nothing ever really went wrong. The only thing that at times worried me was the fact that I did not always remember whether I had disinfected those pliers! But nobody came to any harm . . . that I know of," she chuckled.

Upon Marguerite's retirement, she returned the dental instrument to Doctor Watson's daughter, Beth Radcliffe. "Perhaps I should have put them on display in the museum. Those pliers may well be my only claim to fame!"

Marguerite was born in the Huron County village of Belgrave. She was one of eight children born to Isabelle and J. Alex (Sandy) Young. Her elementary schooling took place in the one-room Belgrave Public School with thirty-five to forty other students. "I guess I was destined to become a teacher from an early age. One morning in Grade 4, I eagerly conducted the opening exercises, filling in for our teacher. I never forgot the wonderful feeling it gave me. I knew then that teaching was my destiny. Throughout my school years, I never doubted my choice of vocation." Marguerite received her teacher's certificate from the London Normal School and taught her first seven years in two rural schools, Lobo Bear Creek School and Biddulph Coursey School, before finally settling into Lucan Public School.

Marguerite's daughters did not follow in Mom's footsteps. They did not choose to enter the teaching or the dental profession.

"The official tooth puller of Lucan Public School," Marguerite McRoberts, **puts her dental pliers to work.**

Terry Culbert's Lucan ~ Home of the Donnellys

Baptism and Hymnbooks

The residents of Lucan have always been a God-fearing, churchgoing lot. They still have four well-attended churches to attest to that. In the village, on a Sunday morning, you have your choice of Anglican, United, or Pentecostal. The Catholic Church is located two miles to the south of the village.

My mother was raised Anglican, my father, United. This was forever a topic of heated discussion in our home because I had yet to be christened. By the time I reached the age of twelve, Dad had won the argument and I was thrust into the fold of the United Church. The morning of my baptism was an embarrassing moment for a boy entering his teens. There at the front of the church, surrounded by parents holding their babies, was the minister, who was a couple of inches shorter than I.

Despite that slightly humiliating experience, I loved going to Lucan United Church, but not necessarily for pious reasons. As an up-and-coming artist, I would search the pews for the newest hymnbooks. On the pristine white front and back inside covers of those books, my artistic talents had free rein. I would draw caricatures of parishioners sleeping, accompanied by the person's name and the date. Of course I drew in ink so the artwork would be around for the next generation to enjoy.

My sister Mary Jane, fifteen years my junior, confided in me that the highlight of her churchgoing memories was finding a hymnal containing one of her big brother's cartoons.

Certificate of Baptism

⌐ This Certifies That ⌐

Terrence Patrick Culbert

Child of *Milward Taylor Culbert*

and his wife, *Mary Elizabeth Patrick*

Born at *London, Ontario*

Date of birth *May 13, 1942.*

Was baptized in *Lucan United Church*

On the *eighth* day of *April*

In the year of our Lord *1955*

in the Name of the Father, and of the Son, and of the Holy Spirit

Witnesses _____

_____

E. M. Cook,
Minister.

Suffer little children, and forbid them not, to come unto me: for of such is the kingdom of heaven. Matthew 19: 14.

AN IRISH NINE, 1922

Part Six: *Village Sports*

Lucan Irish Nine 1922

Photo courtesy University of Western Ontario Archives.

The Famous Irish Nine

Lucan has always been a sports village, and, as with many rural Canadian communities, to this day the favourite game is hockey. However, baseball played a significant part in the village sports history.

The village has been actively playing baseball since 1860. In June of 1885, a baseball club was organized and The Lucan Irish Nine team was born. Befitting their Irish heritage, some of the team members were aptly named: Fife, Stanley, Kenny, O'Neil, Hutchins, Armitage, Jennings, Murdock, and Collins. The team played well and by 1895 they were touring Western Ontario. They travelled by train and by horse-drawn stagecoach with very little downtime in between games. They played a morning game in Exeter, an afternoon game in Goderich, and the following day the team played Clinton on the way home. Out of nineteen games that year, The Irish Nine lost but one.

By 1902, the team had become so successful that many top teams from across Canada and the United States were looking to challenge them. Manager Cabe Hawkshaw was inundated with requests to play his team. Several of the games took place on Lucan's baseball diamond, while others were played in London. That year, with the crack of a bat, the Irish Nine trounced two teams from Detroit, Michigan. Always up for a challenge, on the second of June

1902, they met the well-known and respected Toronto Varsity team at the Lucan ballpark. After fifteen gruelling innings, the Irish broke a tie with Toronto, winning the game 3–2. That string of triumphs was the catalyst for fame. Everyone wanted a piece of the Lucan Irish Nine.

Brenner Brothers Cigar Company of London paid fifty dollars to use the trade name "Famous Irish Nine" for one of their cigar brands. The inside cover of the cigar box displayed a portrait of the handsome team, which included Dick Hodgins, Billie Tripp, Bob Fox, William Porte, Jimmie Anderson, Art Hawkshaw, Doctor Oscar Lang, Cabe Hawkshaw (manager), Cliff Murdy, Fred Smythe, George "Mooney" Gibson, Jesse Tripp, and Angus George.

So popular was the team that often the gate receipts totalled $200 to $250 per game. The club was fairly self-sufficient, to the point where player Jimmie Anderson handcrafted the team's baseball bats in his Lucan woodworking shop.

After a few more successful years, the peak of Lucan's baseball history waned when in 1905 many of the team members dispersed. Angus George, from the Kettle Point First Nation on Lake Huron, left to play professional ball in Toledo, Ohio. Jesse Tripp joined the Varsity team in Toronto, then moved to Weyburn, Saskatchewan, where he became a Member of

The Famous Irish Nine

This is the inside lid of a Brenner Bros. cigar box, circa 1902.
Back row left to right: Dick Hodgins, Billie Tripp, Bob Fox,
William Porte, unknown, Jimmie Anderson
Middle row: Art Hawkshaw, Cabe Hawkshaw,
Doctor Oscar Lang, Cliff Murdy, Fred Smythe
Front row: George Gibson, Jesse Tripp and Angus George.

Parliament. The Irish Nine's star player, George "Mooney" Gibson, left for the United States to catch for the Pittsburg Pirates for twelve years and then for the New York Giants for another two years. Later, Mooney managed the Pittsburgh Pirates and the Chicago Cubs.

In 1902, William Wakefield Revington, the Bard of Biddulph, wrote a much-quoted and very fitting poem:

THE FAMOUS IRISH NINE
All of the local sportsmen here
Have heard of Lucan town;
And of the famous Irish Nine
That's gaining great renown.
They have done well in former years
And this year they did fine;
And proved the best in every test,
The famous Irish Nine.
Once London had a fancy team
As any in the west;
But when they faced the Irish Nine
The Irish proved the best.
But now, they say, to gain the day
Their forces all combine;
Then Toronto tries to win the prize
From our brave Irish Nine.
Toronto University
Has clever boys, they say;
But when they face the Irish Nine
They were not in the play.
They have perhaps some clever chaps,
In fact they all look fine;
But in the field, they have to yield
Before the Irish Nine.
The "Varsity" is a clever team,
Of merry boys the same;
And when they play on any field,
They mostly win the game.
But when they met the Lucan boys,
And all fell into line;
It's then they were defeated,
By the famous Irish Nine.
And now the famous Irish Nine
Will gladly hail the day,
To meet with any local team,
And in a friendly way.
And in the *Globe* and *Free Press*, too
Their manly photos shine;
And who dare say a word today
Against the Irish Nine.

I Could Run Like a Deer

Jean (Morley) Hodgins was raised on her parents' farm near Whalens Corners. As a teenager, she left her family homestead for the bright lights of nearby Lucan and a job as a nursemaid. Her first employment was with the manager of the Bank of Montreal, followed by a position at the home of Mrs. Duncan Ross, and finally working for Beulah Hardy on the outskirts of Lucan.

"Not long after I started working for Beulah, she moved all of us from the farm into the village, as her husband Clarence went overseas fighting in the Second World War. Living in the village gave me the opportunity to search for additional work. I soon secured a part-time job at the creamery."

Even though Jean's days were filled with work, when Beulah asked her to join the Lucan

Lucan Girl's Softball Team (1944-45)

Girls Softball team, Jean was thrilled and immediately agreed to play. "I just loved playing ball, but especially enjoyed the out-of-town games," said Jean. "We would get a ride in the back of Dave Ashworth's pickup truck. He charged each player twenty-five cents for the round trip to Ilderton, Byron, Exeter, or Hensall. Although I wasn't a good hitter, I could run like a deer. I always made it to first base," Jean said proudly. "Jack Murdy, the undertaker, was our coach, and George Ward, the village shoemaker, was our team manager. It was wartime fun."

In 1944, Jean met and married Art Hodgins. "Art was a handsome, baseball-playing, dairy farmer from Clandeboye. I met him at the Stanley Opera House, where all the dances were held. Being wartime, there was always a lack of eligible bachelors. Most of the young women learned to dance together. I remember the first time my friend Lillian Hardy and I saw Art at a dance. He was a fine-looking young man, and we could hardly contain ourselves. We bet each other as to who would date him first. Lillian won the first date, but I won in the long run, marrying Art."

Today, Jean does not quite have the speed of a running deer, but she certainly has not slowed down. She can be seen at all the village functions with camera in hand, snapping photos for the local archives. Over the years, she's become somewhat of a historian. She scans *The Exeter-Times Advocate*, *The London Free Press*, and *The Middlesex Banner*, clipping out anything to do with the Township of Lucan Biddulph. "I must have at least fifty scrapbooks in my library," Jean said. "I'm not interested in giving them to the University of Western

Ontario's archive department. I want them to remain in Lucan. I will donate some of them to the Lucan Area Heritage Donnelly Museum."

"Art was a handsome, baseball-playing, dairy farmer from Clandeboye. I met and married him in 1944," said Jean (Morley) Hodgins.

The Game of Hockey

Before the Lucan Community Centre was constructed, all the village boys, including myself, played hockey either on Shipley's Pond or behind the coal shed at Scott's Elevator. It was always Toronto vs. Montreal, and I was always Turk Broda, the Toronto Maple Leaf goalie, my hockey hero. The arena, completed in 1950, became the envy of many southwestern Ontario municipalities, including the City of London. Thanks to the area's men and women who donated their time and expertise, the Lucan Community Memorial Centre and Arena was completed debt free. The complex was built as a memorial to the Biddulph Township veterans who served Canada during World War II.

With nothing but outdoor rink experience, my buddies and I could suddenly don real uniforms and protective equipment to play organized hockey. I switched from playing goal to playing defence for the Lucan Peewees. Alas, my future as an NHLer came to an abrupt end after a bout with pneumonia. Our family doctor, Clayton George, swiftly administered a penicillin shot and announced that I was not allowed to play hockey for the following three years. From that date on, I no longer played hockey, but was a devoted fan.

I'll never forget the time when the actual Montreal Canadiens played the Lucan Irish Six. It was December 15th, 1952. I was ten years old

and so excited as my father and I entered the arena to watch this much-anticipated exhibition game. It was all and more than I expected it to be. As I watched the play, I became acutely aware of the difference in the sound the professional players' skates made as opposed to the amateurs' skates. Maurice (the Rocket) Richard and Doug Harvey's skates made a deep, positive slicing noise as they whizzed by the stands. The sound I remembered coming off our local players' skates was more of a soft swishing sound. I have never forgotten that very distinct noise generated by the skates of highly skilled professional skaters.

Fred Revington of the Lucan Irish Six played forward that memorable evening. "Our team was very excited about playing the Canadiens and so were the hundreds of fans who packed the arena. Initially, when we were informed that the Canadiens were coming to Lucan, we thought perhaps four or five players would be involved. We never expected the whole team to show up in our arena. It was the experience of a lifetime."

How did the Montreal Canadiens come to play in Lucan? My aunt Muriel's father, Frank Hardy, was a close friend of Dick Irvin, the Montreal Canadiens' coach. They were both pigeon breeders, and Dick Irvin had visited the Hardy farm many times over the years. At the time, the Montreal Canadiens were on a return road trip from Detroit, Michigan, staying at a hotel in London. As a personal favour to his old friend Frank Hardy, Dick brought out his team for a match with the Lucan Irish Six, a fitting event for the arena's new artificial ice pad.

The whole Lucan team met the Canadiens at a reception prior to the game. "The game itself was very interesting," recalls Fred Revington, a retired butcher living in London, Ontario. "During the first period, the Irish Six played the Montreal Canadiens. For the second and third periods, we

Lucan Irish Six — Ontario Intermediate "C" Champions
1953 — 1954

Terry Culbert's Lucan ~ Home of the Donnellys

split up players from both teams. They were an entertaining and great bunch of guys."

The Montreal Canadiens defeated the Boston Bruins in the fifth game to win the Stanley Cup the following spring. A telegram of congratulations was sent to Dick Irvin and his team from the village of Lucan.

Revington's Meat Market and Langford Lumber were proud sponsors of the Irish Six.

Leprechauns on the Ed Sullivan Show

My entertainment as a young boy was centred on various radio programs. I loved listening to *Art Linkletter*, *Amos and Andy*, *Jack Benny*, and *The Green Hornet*. I thought nothing could be better than listening to the radio. It was 1953 and CFPL Television in London had just become the second private station in Canada to begin broadcasting. At the age of eleven, I was exposed to television for the first time. The grainy black and white image transmitted into our living room had our rapt attention. I listened less and less to the radio, as television invaded my visual senses.

In the United States, the *Ed Sullivan Show* went to air on the 20th of June 1948. The American weekly television variety show hosted by Ed Sullivan ran until June 6th 1971. For twenty-three years, Ed Sullivan featured comedians, rock stars, opera singers, ballet dancers, actors, circus acts, trained dogs, and dancing bears. We were privileged to see Elvis Presley, The Beatles, Bob Hope, and Rich Little. The show that excited the residents of Lucan the most took place in 1958. It was Sullivan's annual St. Patrick's Day show, and the boys and girls of the Lucan Leprechauns hockey team travelled to New York City to be part of that show.

The trip was the brainchild of Harold Ribson, the village recreation director and arena manager. A born promoter, he talked the producers of the Ed Sullivan Show into showcasing the Lucan Leprechauns, suggesting the television exposure would be a great boost for minor hockey everywhere.

Larry Lewis was one of the lucky players to make the trip to New York. He was a ten-year-old left-winger at the time. "Most of my friends, including myself, had never even been on an airplane before," he said. "We flew out of London Ontario's Crumlin Airport on a plane belonging to Great Lakes Airline, better known as Great 'Shakes' Airline. It was a turbulent flight, and most of us got sick."

At Toronto's Malton Airport, now Pearson International, the team changed planes, boarding a Trans Canada Air Lines Viscount for the final leg of their trip to New York City. The team was made up of twelve boys, three girls, Harold and Mrs. Ribson, and Bill Smith, the coach. A bus chartered by the New York City Lions Club took them to the Piccadilly Hotel on Broadway. "For all of us kids from Lucan, the Piccadilly Hotel was awe-inspiring, and this was only the beginning. We couldn't get enough of staring out

A portion of the famous Lucan Leprechauns hockey team that appeared on the
1958 Ed Sullivan's St. Patrick's Day show.

the windows and taking in the incredible views. Our rooms were on the top floor of the hotel, and looking out the window, the people down below looked like ants and the cars looked like Dinky Toys. I roomed with Roger Black, Paul Young, and Eddie Harrigan. When we weren't looking out the window, the four of us were jumping from bed to bed having pillow fights."

That afternoon, the team took in the sights of Times Square and then were taken to the CBS Television Studios to watch the rehearsal of the *Ed Sullivan Show*. In a 1958 *Exeter Times-Advocate* essay contest, Leprechaun player Paul Steacy wrote: "The size of the stage and the seating capacity amazed us. From what we had seen on television at home in Lucan, we thought it would be an enormous place, but it was much smaller than we had expected. There were three large TV cameras taking pictures of the show from various angles. Two were mounted on wagon-like affairs while the third was on a crane which could be raised and lowered."

Back at the Piccadilly Hotel, the team readied themselves for the evening show. As their hockey equipment travelled to the studio in a cab, the eighteen Lucanites walked the five blocks. Paul Steacey wrote: "After putting on our uniforms, everyone sat quietly on the stairway waiting for the big moment. While sitting there, we spent a few minutes talking to actress Mitzi Gaynor, another guest."

Standing in the wings, they heard Ed Sullivan introduce them: "Right here on our stage, the champion peewee hockey team of Canada, the Lucan Leprechauns. Give these youngsters from Ontario, Canada, a big hand!"

As the group nervously filed out onto the stage, Ed Sullivan shook each person's hand individually. "It was all over in a few minutes. It was very exciting, and we were all hoping our parents and friends back home had been able to see us. After the show, we kept Ed and Irish actress Maureen O'Hara busy signing autographs. We found them very friendly," wrote Paul Steacy in his essay.

The next morning, as they made their way to breakfast, the young hockey players were astounded to see before them the entire Montreal Canadien hockey team. The young boys were in awe to be in such close proximity of their heroes. "It turned out they'd played a game the night before at Madison Square Gardens and were staying in our hotel," Larry Lewis explained. The Leprechauns' final event was a visit to Madison Square Gardens.

Paul Steacy's second-prize essay concludes with: "We had only been away thirty-six hours, but so much had happened that it seemed much longer. This was an experience we will not forget for the rest of our lives, and the 'Luck of the Irish' was truly with us."

Woman Hockey Announcer

While in Lucan, I stopped at Scott's Elevator to purchase a new pair of work boots. My old ones were cracked and worn, resulting in wet feet when it rained. Mary Jane Van Kasteren, the office manager for the farm supplies division, served me. Selling me the boots became secondary as the friendly, talkative woman told me she not only had a passion for hockey, but was the home game announcer for Lucan's Junior "D" team, the Lucan Irish. I had grown up with radio and Saturday night hockey and I have never forgotten the incredulous voice of Foster Hewitt screaming over the airwaves: "He shoots . . . he scores!" Mary Jane is not Foster Hewitt. Firstly, she is a female, and secondly, she does not broadcast on radio, but she is a hockey announcer.

Mary Jane explained: "When Ann Hardy retired as the Junior 'D' announcer, I was asked if I had time to help out. Wendy Hardy, Anne's cousin, is the timekeeper and wanted someone to fill out the game sheets, play warm-up music, and announce the goals and penalties. I couldn't say no to this opportunity. It sounded like great fun. I very quickly got into the routine. During any stoppage in the game, we play music to pump up the fans. It keeps them excited and increases the energy level inside the arena. We have a great musical library of thirty-second clips from groups such as Queen. 'We are the Champions' and 'Thunder' are of course the two songs everyone knows, and the fans really react to. The Lucan Irish team is made up of young men sixteen to twenty-one years old. They play Belmont, Parkhill, Exeter, Tavistock, and Thamesford. Sometimes I travel to out-of-town games during the playoffs, but only as a spectator, which is a nice change for me."

As a teenager, Mary Jane played defence for the Lucan Leprechauns, the intermediate girls' team. Born Mary Jane Martens, she was one of nine children raised on a dairy farm near Bryanston. In 1995, she formed the Lucan Junior Girls' team, made up of seven- to thirteen-year-olds. Today she coaches the Lucan Intermediate Girls, aged seventeen to twenty-one. Her team won the Intermediate "C" Provincial Championship for 2004–05. She loves coaching the young women and finds it very rewarding.

Mary Jane's husband, Roy, is also an avid hockey fan. Like his wife, he grew up on a dairy farm and played hockey as a child. Roy is the service manager at Stratford Farm Equipment and coaches the Lucan Shamrocks, a midget team. Hockey is very much part of their family life. Starting all of their four children playing by the age of five, Mary Jane and Roy got involved with their children's teams by coaching and being part of the teams' executive.

I think you'd be hard-pressed to find a woman in the role of a hockey announcer anywhere in Canada. "Being an arena hockey announcer is lots of fun, and I just love it!" When asked if she has ever felt vulnerable behind the glass, she smiled: "I have never felt that I was in danger of being hit by a puck or high stick. I have seen the glass break along the boards, but fortunately not near the timekeeper's booth. Perhaps the glass is thicker in our area!"

Kentucky of the North

The horse has been a fixture on the Lucan scene forever. It was there for the first pioneers, for the stagecoaches, for the local doctor, and for pulling the undertaker's funeral wagon or sleigh. The horse was there for the milkman and the bread man and for delivering freight from the rail station. The horse was there for recreation, racing, and almost everything else.

Lucan's first racetrack was established around 1910. Box stalls for twelve horses and a grandstand for over 200 spectators were erected. Records from the harness industry show that the Lucan racetrack held three races in 1920 and two in 1923. The sport of harness racing in the Township of Lucan Biddulph runs deep. The area is often referred to as the "Kentucky of the North" in United States racing circles.

CLINT HODGINS

Clint Hodgins, a good friend of my father's, was born in 1907, two miles to the west of Lucan, on a farm near the hamlet of Clandeboye. Horses and racing were a natural for young Clint. His father, "Racer Sid" Hodgins, a driver and trainer, raced at local fairs. At the age of twenty-one, Clint left the family farm to embark on a long and successful career in harness racing, primarily in the United States.

In 1940, Clint captured a string of world records with a two-year-old trotting filly named Acrasia. Clint's greatest fame came in the post-war years as the driver of Proximity. This great trotting mare rewrote the record book between 1948 and 1950. After driving the world's two fastest pacers in 1959, Clint was named best driver of the year.

The Biddulph native winter trained in Orlando, Florida, for decades. As a driver, Clint was poised and nerveless, with an uncanny sense of timing, earning him nose and head victories on late rushes. Many young horsemen, including William "Buddy" Gilmore of Lucan, credit Clint Hodgins with boosting their careers, claiming he was the greatest teacher of all time. In 1972, Clint bred, raised, trained, and drove Skipper Thorpe, an outstanding three-year-old pacer, to win eight stakes, giving him a 1:58.2 mark.

Clint was inducted into the United States Hall of Fame in Goshen, New York, in 1973, and Canada's Hall of Fame in 1977.

When Clint retired from driving, he followed his homebred colts and fillies around in the summer to the Ontario Sires Stakes. He was a wonderful philanthropist, giving over $1.5 million to charities in his hometown area. Clint Hodgins died in 1979 after suffering a stroke. He was only seventy-two years of age.

Clint Hodgins driving Proximity. This great trotting mare rewrote the record book in 1948 and 1950.

Neil McRann wearing his green and white shamrock silks.

William "Buddy" Gilmour, a Canadian and United States Hall of Fame inductee.

NEIL McRANN

Even though Neil McRann's father raced horses at local tracks during the 1930s and '40s, Neil did not seem interested in the sport as young boy. That all changed in 1951, when he caught the bug and began driving at fall fairs and at Old Woodbine Racetrack in Toronto. Ten years later, when night racing began at London's Western Fair Raceway, Neil became a serious contender. He had a lot of success raising and training pacers and trotters. In 1971, Neil purchased a trotter named Dart Camp from Dr. Lawrence Haryett of London. During the horse's lengthy career, Dart Camp made it to the winner's circle seventy times, earning close to $480,000.

Neil was particularly proud of his Irish heritage and displayed shamrocks on his green and white silks. He was named to the Western Fair Raceway's Wall of Fame in June of 1985. Over his thirty-year career, Neil won more than 800 races and earned more than $1.5 million. His peers regarded him as "one of the nicest guys in the business."

WILLIAM "BUDDY" GILMOUR

William Douglas Gilmour was born on the outskirts of Lucan on the 23rd of July 1932. Clint Hodgins taught the teenager, known as "Buddy," the art of harness racing. In the early fifties, Buddy worked the Buffalo–Batavia, New York State circuit. With 165 victories in 1959, he won his first and only driving title. Over the next three decades, his wins and purse money grew. Buddy's greatest financial success was in 1984, earning an outstanding $4.4 million. During his long and successful career, Buddy won 5,380 races and over $44 million in purse money. William "Buddy" Gilmour was a Canadian Hall of Fame inductee in 1988 and a United States Hall of Fame inductee in 1990. Explaining his driving skills, Buddy Gilmour said: "It's just something you have a feeling for. There's a communication between the horse and rider that is hard to explain."

JUBILEE GRATTON

Standard-bred Jubilee Gratton was born in Lucan in 1927, Canada's Jubilee year. Don and Bill Banting owned the mare. They were sons of Dr. W.T. Banting, a Lucan family physician for fifty-two years. Dr. Banting used the horse to take him through snow-blocked country roads to see sick patients. She was a faithful horse; however, at times she would get impatient waiting for the doctor, returning home without him. The lone horse trotting through the streets was not an uncommon sight. Actually, Bill Banting trained the horse on the streets of Lucan. Finally, on the 23rd of May 1957, Jubilee Gratton, then a good-looking thirty-year-old, out-raced her stablemate, Miss Barbara Ann Lee, at the opening of the new Lucan Racetrack situated behind the Community Centre.

In 1960, the *Exeter Times Advocate* ran a picture I shot of Jubilee Gratton and Bill Banting, claiming that the horse at thirty-three years of age was still eating corn off the cob. That same year, *The Canadian Sportsman* wrote

My father shot this photograph of his good friend Clint Hodgins and me in 1957, when the world-class harness racing champion was back in Lucan for holidays.

an article on Jubilee Gratton entitled: "Lucan's Oldest Standard Bred."

Lucan is still a hotbed of harness racing. New and eager owners, trainers, and drivers flourish in and around the village.

Jubilee Gratton became Lucan's oldest horse in 1960. "At thirty-three years of age," said her trainer Bill Banting, "she is still eating corn off the cob."

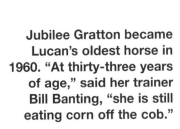

Wall of Fame

The Wall of Fame was created in 1977 to recognize the men and women who have made an outstanding contribution to Western Fair Harness Racing. Photographs of all the past inductees line the walls at the Top of the Fair concourse of the Western Fair Raceway in London, Ontario. In 1977, Bill Herbert became the first inductee for his contributions as an owner, driver, and breeder of Standard bred horses. His son Jack Herbert was inducted a few years later.

On the 27th of May 2000, Lucan brothers Jack and Norm Hardy were honoured as inductees to the Wall of Fame for their lifelong contributions. "We've worked, rode, trained, and owned horses all our lives," said Norm. "Every Wednesday afternoon, Dad would take us to a small-town racetrack in places like Strathroy, Exeter, and Goderich. During the summer holidays and in the fall, away we'd go again. Racing horses was a hobby in those days."

It was Jack's and Norm's long-time friend Neil McRann (Wall of Fame 1985) who introduced the brothers to the sport of harness racing. It started innocently enough when Neil brought a colt to Norm's farm to be raised and trained. Norm and his brother Jack took an immediate interest in the horse and everything connected with harness racing. Norm explained: "As the horse got older, I'd put lines on her

halter and we would run together every night. There was no sulky cart; I was running with the mare trotting ahead of me. We did this for over a month until she could run farther than I could. All that exercise was of great benefit and when hockey season began in the fall, I was in marvellous shape."

In 1955, Jack and Norm bought their first racehorse, "Pauline Volo," for $825. "I didn't have my half of the purchase price and had to borrow the money from Jack," said Norm. "My wife, Lena, wasn't pleased, and that's putting it mildly. At the time, we were newlyweds without a bathroom or furnace in the house. She felt I was squandering our hard-earned money, which she insisted could have been put to better use. I didn't necessarily disagree with her, but by this time the racing bug had bit both Jack and me. We raced Pauline Volo any chance we got until she was forced into retirement at age fourteen. In those days, big racing money didn't exist. We'd win fifty, sometimes a hundred dollars per heat. During her career, though, Pauline Volo won sixty-three races and banked earnings of $28,661; more than enough to pay for a bathroom and furnace," smiled Norm.

Jack and Norm were owner-trainers, not drivers. For years, the brothers depended on their friends Neil McRann, Clarence Young, and Levi "Jiggs" McFadden to do the driving for them.

Jack and Norm raised and raced a lot of successful horses and each had his personal favourite. Jack was extremely fond of a chestnut gelding named "Dwac." Dwac went on to win twenty-four races, earning a total of $72,186. Norm's preferred performer was "Robust King," although it was a bay gelding called "Kent Express" that had the most impact on his life. Under wet conditions, Kent Express would always break stride and finish last. However, one sloppy Saturday afternoon, Kent Express and five other horses went to the post in the $2,100 preferred handicap race. With 8:1 odds, Kent Express surprised everyone by finishing the one-mile race a length ahead of the other horses in a time of 2:14.2, paying $18.90 to win, $12.70 to place, and $6.80 to show.

Eventually, Jack's and Norm's sons Andy and Ken would become drivers. Norm's son Ken started training horses at the age of nine. By the time he was eighteen years old, he was driving at the Western Fair Raceway. On his very first meet, he was one drive short of winning "the best driver of the meet." At age nineteen, he accomplished that feat.

Ken's son Glen, along with his wife, Mary, are very active in the horse business. Their daughter Carolyn at eighteen months loved to ride in a car seat with Great-Grandpa Norm as he drove his truck around the track, jogging the horses. If Carolyn should decide to make a hobby or career of horses, she will become the fifth generation on Norm's side of the family.

Jack's son Andy not only trains his own horses but others as well. His daughter-in-law Ann and granddaughter Amy are also involved in the sport. This makes four generations of the Jack Hardy family involved in harness racing.

"Racing is a hobby for us," said Jack. "We tried to make it pay and we succeeded. However, our main reason for getting into horse racing was for the love of the sport, and that has never changed."

Rugby Twins

My introduction to the game of rugby took place over a quarter century ago in Edinburgh, Scotland. I was on a trip to the UK with my old friend Joe Cote, a CBC Radio broadcaster with a passion for rugby. The first game we saw was an international "test match" on December 9th, 1978. Scotland was facing "the warriors of rugby from Down Under," the New Zealand All Blacks, at Edinburgh's Murrayfield. In front of a damp but cheerful crowd of 70,000, New Zealand slogged through the mist on a well-grassed but slippery pitch to defeat Scotland 18 to 9. The following week we visited Cardiff, Wales, to watch New Zealand take on the Barbarians at the Arms Park. The Barbarians is an all-star team, traditionally chosen from the best players in England, Scotland, Wales, Ireland, and France. December 16th dawned clear and cold with a sharp northeast wind. Most of the 47,500 fans were Welshmen singing their hearts out as the New Zealand All Blacks won again with a score of 18 to 16.

Having grown up as a spectator of hockey and baseball, this was a new and exciting sport for me. Definition of Rugby from *Collier's 1997 Encyclopaedia*: "Rugby is a type of football game, taking its name from the English public preparatory school. Derived from soccer or association football, rugby in turn was the forerunner of North American football. Kicking and dribbling with the foot are a part of rugby; however, continuous passing of the ball is its most characteristic feature. The object of the game is for each side to attempt to ground the ball beyond their opponent's goal line and score the greater number of points within two forty-minute periods of play."

When a pair of athletic twin brothers from Lucan started Grade 9 at Medway High School in Arva, their football coach recommended they try out for the rugby team. After a few practices, Mike and Dan Pletch knew that rugby was their sport. For the next five years, the lads played rugby for the Medway Cowboys. By the time the twins reached Grade 11, they realized that working out with weights would make them even more effective athletes. They won tournaments in Ohio and New York City. At an OFSSA (Ontario Federation of Secondary School Athletics) tournament in Barrie, the Medway Cowboys placed third, the best placing the school had ever achieved.

Mike and Dan were born in London, Ontario, on April 12th, 1983, to Connie and Don Pletch. After eight years in Ilderton, the family built a house southwest of Lucan. The boys loved sports from an early age, playing hockey, baseball, and soccer. After graduation from Medway High School, Mike and Dan enrolled at McMaster University in Hamilton, Ontario.

Mike's goal is to become a civil engineer and eventually to open his own consulting firm. Dan is enrolled in an honours geography program with a minor in business. He is planning to become a high school teacher or, should teaching not work out, an urban planner.

It didn't take the twins long to join the McMaster Marauders rugby team. They have won the Ontario University Championships two years in a row. "Since we joined the team, it has turned around," said Mike. "Not that we can take all the credit—there are a lot of good players at McMaster. However, being twins, we are a bit of a novelty. We get lots of attention from the *London Free Press* and the New PL television station in London. We've heard stories that opposing team members don't realize there are two of us on the field. One comment was: "That guy must be in really good shape; he seems to be everywhere at the same time," laughed Dan. When asked if they have been seriously hurt in any of their games, Dan recalls a time when his ear was almost ripped off. After wrapping his head in tape, he went back to finish the match. It was only after he went to the hospital that he realized the severity of his injury, requiring eight stitches to put the ear back in place. Brother Mike has been fairly lucky so far, his one injury being a separated shoulder.

Not only do the boys play for the McMaster Marauders, but since the age of fifteen, every summer they have played for the London St. George team. They have advanced to the men's team, playing clubs from Windsor, Brampton, and Burlington. Mike and Dan have played four national championships, winning three silver medals and a gold in 2003 against British Columbia. They have played in Chile, Italy, and England. "The British always give us a special, warm welcome. Our styles are quite different and we learn from each other," explained Mike. "We play the front row as props. It is a technical position, and by the time we are thirty years of age, we will be at the peak of our game, knowing all the tricks."

At five feet eleven inches, they are maintaining their ideal body weight of 240 pounds. How much longer will they be able to play this very physically demanding sport? Even though the brothers know men in their fifties still playing, they told me they don't think they will hang in that long. But somehow I feel their involvement with rugby will continue long after they stop actively playing the game.

The rugby playing Pletch brothers.

Kaschper Racing Shells

On Saintsbury Line, just north of Highway 4, sits a nondescript structure looking much like a large storage shed. It is anything but. Behind those walls are experts at work building world-class racing boats. This is home to Kaschper Racing Shells. Jakob Kaschper, the founder, is not only a designer and builder of boats, but he and his associates row, coach, and regularly race their newest equipment in order to gather performance information. From Olympic athlete to recreational rower, Jakob continues to produce and refine his racing shells to serve his customers' needs.

Jakob Kaschper learned his trade at the Bootswerft Empacher in Germany under the personal tutelage of Willy Empacher, a skilled and experienced boat builder. In 1958, Jakob immigrated to Canada, but never lost his close communication with his teacher and mentor. After moving to London, Ontario, Jakob joined the London Rowing Club and became an active oarsman. Upon discovering that the club was in need of equipment, he promptly began building boats for them in an old barn on Lake Fanshawe. In 1961, Jakob built the first short fifty-eight-foot shell. The average length of eights at that time was sixty-two feet. Shortening the shell by four feet reduced the friction and drag by reducing the wetted surface.

Jakob began production in the landlocked village of Lucan in 1969. Much of the first year was spent producing moulds and tooling for rowing shells, from singles to the large eights. The earliest shells were made of Spanish cedar veneer, form-laminated under vacuum pressure. Known as vac-shells, these are still being used worldwide.

Designing and building boats has always been Jakob's first love. One of his designs in 1980 was a new non-wooden shell called "tiger stripe," which has a black semi-transparent carbon glass hull. This design proved very popular. The Ontario Science Centre took a tiger stripe on a high-tech exhibition that toured Canada. The Canadian National Women's Team rowed a tiger stripe eight at the world championships in Munich, Germany. Weighing only 198 pounds, it was the lightest sectional eight at the competition.

All wooden rowing shells were replaced by the monocoque shell in 1990. Made of a carbon-honeycombed material, it is lighter, stronger, and stiffer, and also reduces maintenance. There are many variables in hull design: shape, weight, and corresponding drag. The greatest change has occurred in the evolution of composite materials, giving rise to lighter and stiffer equipment.

Always looking for an edge, master boat builder Jakob introduced his Wing Rigger Line of Kaschper Racing Shells in 1996. He is interested in providing optimal equipment to make the most of rowers' output. Throughout all his years of building and designing racing shells, Jakob is holding true to his company creed:

Kaschper Racing Shells will never stop at

just reaching the competitive edge . . . We go for platinum in production so you can go for gold on the water.

www.kaschper.com

Photos courtesy Kaschper Racing Shells Ltd.

**Xeno Muller, Olympic Champion
1996 Gold
2000 Silver**

**Mike Fogeron, the 1992 Olympic Gold Medal winner
of the Men's Eight, is pictured to the left of
master boat builder Jakob Kaschper.**

**Eberbach, Germany, December 10, 2004
Grand opening of the Kaschper-Europe showroom.**

Lucan Homing Pigeon Club

In 1927, an Englishman named Frank Hardy helped to found the Canadian Racing Pigeon Union in London, Ontario. Three years later, he founded the Lucan Homing Pigeon Club in the village where he lived. Frank was far from being a pigeon novice, as he and his friends had raised pigeons as boys back in England. At the age of sixteen, Frank took employment with a man who was involved in pigeon racing. During this period, Frank became very knowledgeable about the intricacies of the bird.

In 1912, Frank immigrated to Canada and after arriving in London, Ontario, he worked as a butcher. His dream was to be self-employed, and before long he opened his own slaughterhouse and butcher shop in the village of Lucan. Shortly thereafter, he met and married Violet Shoebotham, and the couple raised nine children.

Neither work nor his family ever seemed to get in the way of Frank's passion for pigeon racing. After reading an advertisement in a local paper, Frank bought his first pigeons. According to his son Norm: "Dad purchased the pigeons from an Ottawa student who was moving back home. There were eight birds in total, both male and female of the Moser strain, named after Herman Moser, a famous bird breeder living in Aurora, Illinois. When Dad brought them home to Lucan, he constructed a pigeon coop at the rear of his garage."

Almost immediately, Frank's sons, Clarence, Jack, Norm, and Harry, showed an interest in the sport. Jack and Norm built coops behind their father's slaughterhouse, while Clarence erected his in an adjoining field. When Clarence went overseas during World War II, Jack and Norm looked after his pigeons. "When Jack and I were boys," said Norm, "we carried our young birds further and further from the coop each day, creating our own miniature races.

"I remember my parents bringing some pigeon eggs home from a trip to England. The eggs were given to Dad by the manager of the Queen's Loft, a Royal Pigeon Racing Association. Dad eventually produced three stock birds. Quite often my father showed his birds at The Royal Agricultural Winter Fair in Toronto, where he also acted as a judge on occasion."

In 1935, Frank Hardy entered CU1932#177 in a 1,000-mile race from Oklahoma City to Lucan. The three-year-old bird flew the distance in three days, eight hours and eighteen minutes, winning the race, to the delight of the Hardy family.

Frank Hardy died in 1965 at the age of seventy-one doing something he felt very passionate about. He had just completed a speech at the pigeon union banquet and was still on his feet when he collapsed of heart failure. A few months later, his wife, Violet, was named a past honorary member of the Canadian Racing Pigeon Union. Women were and still are active in pigeon racing.

Frank's son Clarence became president of both the Southwestern Ontario Federation and the Lucan Homing Pigeon Club. In the late 1960s, the Lucan Club held its first large banquet. The formal occasion saw men dressed in their Sunday best, while the women wore long, stylish gowns. This popular dinner banquet became an annual event for the next ten years.

A 500-mile memorial award was created in memory of Frank Hardy. After his son Clarence's death in 1995, the award was renamed The Hardy Memorial 500-Mile Race. This annual race begins in Grand-Mère, Quebec. If a pigeon fancier wishes to enter the race, his or her bird must be able to fly 700 miles or more. Norm Hardy's male pigeon named "Gretzky" CU1993#9935 has won the Hardy Memorial trophy several times over its lifetime.

Nowadays, pigeons are transported long distances by a fifth-wheel pickup truck and trailer. The trailers hold forty to fifty birds in specially designed compartments, making it easy to feed and water the birds. The transporters will stop and pick up pigeons at various clubhouses en route to the race destination. Each bird wears a tiny computerized microchip on its leg, which registers automatically on a footpad as the homing pigeon returns to its coop at the end of a long-distance race.

Pigeon racing is still in the Hardy blood. Clarence's son Tom, along with his uncles Jack and Norm, are still involved wholeheartedly. However, Norm Hardy would love to have more young people participating in the sport. He was very pleased when two teenagers, along with their fathers, joined the Lucan Club in 2003. So far, all four are still enthusiastic about this old-fashioned sport.

**Frank Hardy, a founding member of the
Canadian Racing Pigeon Union (1927), and his wife, Violet.**

**Norm and Lena Hardy inspect one of their racing pigeons
outside their backyard coop.**

PART SEVEN: *Village Music*

Johnny Cash playing at the Lucan Arena for the second time.
The author was nineteen when he took this unpublished photograph.

Music in the Village

My musical career ended before it ever began. I suffered two major pitfalls, effectively ending any aspirations I might have had. My foray into music occurred when I was an aspiring seven-year-old soprano. Encouraged and accompanied by my Grade 2 teacher, Mrs. Muriel Cobleigh, I was entered in the Kirkton Garden Party's semi-final singing competition in Kirkton, Ontario.

Situated on Highway 23 between Lucan and Mitchell, the tiny village was home to the first Timothy Eaton's store in Canada. The day of the competition, Mrs. Cobleigh played the piano, I sang my heart out, and won the semi-finals. I was basking in glory, which unfortunately was to be short lived. Only a couple of months later, I had to sing at the finals. I practiced endlessly, much to the annoyance of my sister Dana. When the big day arrived, I walked up the steps of the Kirkton Fall Fair band shell, taking my place at centre stage. As Mrs. Cobleigh played, I sang two, possibly three lines and then it happened. I suddenly noticed the large audience, everyone looking at me with great expectation. I froze! Not a sound escaped my lips. It was over! The end of a promising singing career. Dejected and embarrassed, I left the stage.

My next foray into music took place five years later. I had decided to become a drummer. Auditions were held in the Anglican Church Hall for a village orchestra. I entered the audition, proudly setting up my snare drum on its stand. The instrument had belonged to my Great-Uncle Ted Player, a soldier and drummer in the Boer War. As I proceeded to play with all my heart, an irate music teacher stormed across the floor claiming I could not keep the beat. He took the sticks from my hands attempting to show me how the drum should be played. He beat my beautiful family heirloom with such force that it crashed to the floor. Devastated, I swept up the antique snare drum and left the building, not to return for many years.

However, my passion for music was too strong to be put off by those early experiences. I attended musical events and concerts whenever I possibly could. I became a keen observer instead of a participant. When I learned that country singer Johnny Cash was coming to the Lucan Arena on his first visit to Canada, I was thrilled and bought a ticket. I was sixteen years old and had just purchased my first quality still camera. The night of the show, I was fortunate to take a photograph of Johnny Cash signing autographs in front of his dressing-room door.

Two years later, on Johnny's second visit to Lucan, I carried a sixteen-by-twenty-inch enlargement of that photo to the arena. I approached his bodyguard asking if Johnny would autograph the photo for me. "Give me a

I photographed Johnny Cash signing autographs in the Lucan Arena on his first visit to Canada. I was sixteen years of age at the time. Two years later, when he returned, I got him to sign an enlargement of the picture. Mr. Cash hired me to shoot candid shots that night and in Guelph the next evening. This is the first time these photographs have ever been published.

**Johnny Western wrote and sang
"The Ballad of Paladin"
for the hit television series,
*Have Gun, Will Travel***

**Canada's first topless rock band,
The Bare Ones,
played at the Orange Shillelagh.**

second, I'll see what I can do!" A few moments later, to my surprise, he said: "Mr. Cash wants to see you, son!" He ushered me into the dressing room to meet the "Man in Black." Johnny liked the picture I'd taken two years earlier and asked me to shoot his concert that evening as well as

the concert in Guelph the following night. I was elated and excited! My first brush with a famous performer.

On stage with Johnny Cash in Lucan was a man called Johnny Western. He was a featured guitarist and Cash's master of ceremonies on all the road trips. Western was a songwriter who made a name for himself writing and singing "The Ballad of Paladin" for CBS Television's popular Western series, *Have Gun, Will Travel*.

In those days, the Lucan Arena was one of the best concert venues in southwestern Ontario. Over the next few years, Lucan would host many of North America's top names in popular music. I was in the audience listening to Marty Robbins and on two occasions saw the Everly brothers, Don and Phil, perform.

In the late 1960s, as a young news cameraman for CFPL Television, I received the plum assignment of filming The Bare Ones at the Lucan's Orange Shillelagh tavern. These four women were billed as Canada's first topless rock band, and I had gone to high school with Dawn, one of the band members. It was an interesting evening for a young man, and to top it off, I was able to obtain an autographed picture of the band.

The first Music Festival was held in 1956, growing from an idea at a Home and School Association meeting. Ruth Acheson and Beulah Hardy were the organizers. The name was changed to The North Middlesex Music Festival, and on many occasions I shot pictures of the festival winners for the *Exeter Times Advocate* newspaper.

Lucan has had a long history of performing bands. During the '20s, '30s, and '40s, dance bands regularly played in our village. In 1923, Joseph Benn, a violin-playing farmer, got together with Roland Hodgins on piano, Homer Lewis on drums, and George Nangle playing saxophone, forming The Shamrock Orchestra. Joseph's sister Barbara Benn played the piano and chorded along to her brother's violin. When

they played at square dances, Hugh Toohey, "Caller of the Irish Dance," would join them.

The Shamrock Orchestra was popular during the 1920s and throughout the depression years of the 1930s. Those were financially tough times for everyone. The only time the band received a monetary reward was when someone passed around the hat. During the 1940s, songs such as "The White Cliffs of Dover" and "When the Lights Go on Again All over the World" were great crowd favourites, creating a feeling of patriotism in Biddulph Township. Unfortunately, The Shamrock Orchestra folded in 1947. Joe Benn and his sister Barbara continued to play at square dances along with their friend Hugh Toohey.

Another popular band in the 1930s was the Flanagan Orchestra, originally known as the Avalon Orchestra. The small group of men from northwest of Lucan played in Detroit, Kitchener, Seaforth, Centralia, and Mooresville, as well as Lucan. The orchestra consisted of pianist Dick Neil, Walter Dobbs on violin, and the talented Leo Flanagan on drums, mouth organ, piano, and violin.

Unable to read music because he had never taken lessons, Leo was blessed with a tremendous ear, teaching himself by listening to the radio. A lot of his new material was gained from the Don Messer radio program. Other members over the years were drummer Jack Hotson, saxophonist Horace Mason, guitarist "Shorty" Sovereign, and pianist Miss O'Donnell.

In 1938, the George Nangle Orchestra was formed. The band's slogan was: "Dingle and Dangle with George Nangle." Eventually, George quit and an experienced band member

The Adam Brock Orchestra
was popular at the beginning
of the Second World War.

Tales of the Donnelly Feud (1979)
were written and sung by
"Canada's Singing Cowboy,"
Earl Heywood.

The Canadian Playboys were
regulars at Lucan Arena dances.
This photo was taken in 1957.

named Adam Brock took over as the leader. The Adam Brock Orchestra played dance music in Kincardine, Ipperwash and Sauble Beach, Hyde Park, Lakeside near St. Mary's, and at home in Lucan. In 2004, I visited my father's old friend Clarence Haskett, a retired funeral director and a former drummer in the orchestra. I asked him to share his memories with me.

"Every Tuesday evening for over a year we could be heard on London's CFPL Radio," recalled Clarence. "The host was Hartley McVicar. He would introduce our band, letting the radio audience know where they could see us playing live. If the Lionel Thornton Orchestra of London had too many bookings, they'd call us in to help out." Drummer Haskett left Adam Brock's Orchestra in 1943 to go overseas with the Argyle Southern Highlanders.

The well-known Lucan Male Choir was organized in the 1940s under the direction of Mrs. Harold Sturgis. Over the years, they sang on local radio, at church services, and at the Middlesex Seed Fair. During the Second World War, they were instrumental in raising money for Victory Bonds. Through "Booster Nights," the orchestra helped to finance the Lucan Memorial Community Centre in memory of the brave young people who lost their lives fighting for freedom overseas.

The female version of the Lucan Male Choir, the "Singing Sister Trio," was made up of the Hardy sisters: Muriel, Lillian, and Dorothy. They entertained and delighted audiences during the 1940s. Muriel and Lillian sang soprano, while their youngest sister, Dorothy, sang alto. The young women never rehearsed. "Being sisters, we had close harmony," Dorothy

Revington said. Her sister Muriel Culbert added, "We received good training in the Anglican Church choir and were genetically predisposed, as our parents had wonderful singing voices. But fame comes with a price," laughed Muriel. "The day our brother Jack married Helen, we had to leave midway through the wedding. We were booked to sing in front of an audience of 3,000 people at the Farm Show in London. After the performance ended, we quickly left, drove back to Lucan, and rejoined the festivities."

The Donnelly history also left its mark on the Lucan music scene. Tribute songs were composed and sung about the Donnellys over the years. Country singer-composer Earl Heywood of Wingham, Ontario, produced an entire album in 1979 entitled *Tales of the Donnelly Feud*. The following stanza is from one of Heywood's songs:

> *Six men were charged with murder*
> *The jury listened for a while,*
> *As O'Conner told his story*
> *At the Donnelly murder trial.*
> *A new trial was re-ordered*
> *When all would not agree,*
> *And still the final verdict read*
> *"Not Guilty—you go free."*

Stompin' Tom Connors, one of Canada's most popular and prolific singer-songwriters, composed two Donnelly songs for his compact disc *Stompin' Tom Sings Canadian History*. Connors's compositions include "The Black Donnellys Massacre" and "Jenny Donnelly."

Despite my own dismal failure in the music world, music in Lucan not only survived but left a significant impact on village history.

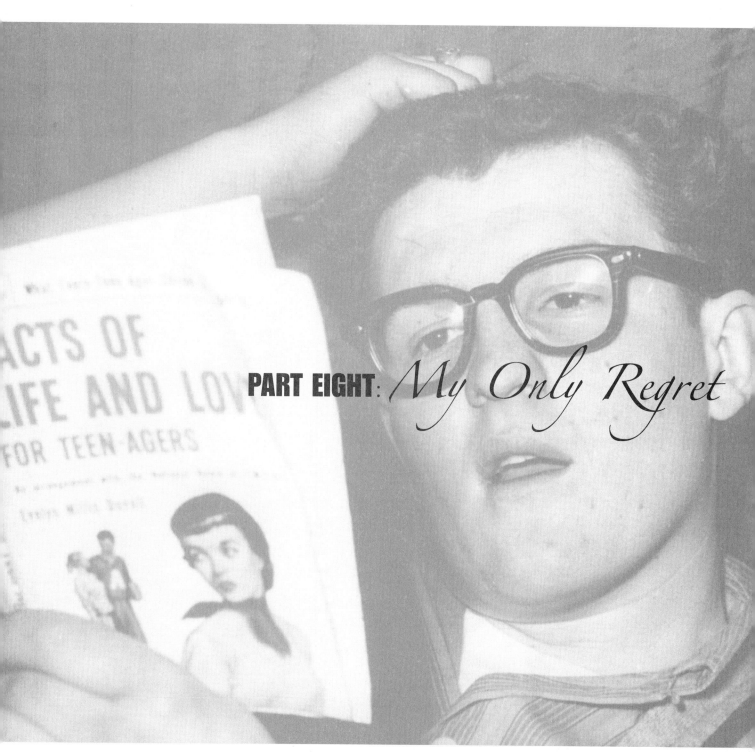

ACTS OF
LIFE AND LOV
FOR TEEN-AGERS

PART EIGHT: *My Only Regret*

Photograph of the author at seventeen by his sister Dana.

My Only Regret

The author with Anne Revington

LaVerne George

Rose Revington

Beth Watson

Bonnie Drennan

Growing up in Lucan, I missed out on a very important life experience. To my great frustration, I was never able to woo a girlfriend, despite my charm and good looks (or so I thought). I was seven or eight when I asked a girl out for the very first time. Anne was a pretty, blonde, older girl. She was a head taller than I and a year older. When I went to call on her, Anne's teenage brothers teased us mercilessly. The relationship did not last very long; but I had set a standard for years to come.

The village was blessed with an abundance of gorgeous girls who turned into beautiful teenagers. There were Anne, her sister Rose, Beth, LaVerne, Judy, Heather, Marie, Margaret, Bonnie, Carol, and her sister Joan. Some of my friends dated the local lasses, but this cute, cuddly, albeit chubby, guy was plain out of luck.

I travelled six miles to Granton, only to be rejected by Marnie. I was eighteen and working full-time at CFPL Television in London; I was driving a bank-owned, brand-new 1961 Austin Healey bug-eyed Sprite. Pulling up to Marnie's home with the top down, I mustered up the courage to ask her to go for a drive in the country. It wasn't to be. Her excuse: "Mom said that I've got to finish my homework!"

Then, out of the blue, Julia of Saintsbury Line seemed to take an interest in me, or perhaps it was my sleek green sports car. Courting Julia lasted a couple of months, ending shortly after she started university. She dumped me for a football player.

Had only one of those beautiful young women agreed to marry me, there would be more Culberts *Lingering Longer in Lovely Lucan* today!

Heather Acheson and Judy Haskett   **Joan and Carol Young**

Margaret Eizenga　　　**Marie Whitehead**

Postcard sent by the author to his colleagues at CFPL TV.

Julia Crozier

Marnie Ellis

References

Fazakas, Ray. 1977. *The Donnelly Album: The complete and authentic account illustrated with photographs of Canada's famous feuding family.* Toronto: McMillan of Canada.

Fazakas, Ray. 2001. *In search of the Donnellys.* Hamilton: Self-published.

Finlayson, William D., Robert J. Pearce, Peter A. Timmins, & Bern Wheeler, The London Museum of Archaeology. 1990. *London, Ontario: The first 11,000 years.* London: Webco Publications.

Lapp, Eula C. 1980. *China was my university: The life of Hulda May (Culbert) Carscallen.* Agincourt: Generation Press.

Lewis, Jennie Raycraft. 1967. *The luck of Lucan.* London: Sprint Publishing.

Manure fuels power project. 2004. *London Free Press* 10/26.

Mulhall, Mary. 1996. *Lucan and Lucanians: A revised history of Lucan.* Lucan, County Dublin, Ireland: Self-published.

Perkel, Colin N. 2002. *Well of lies: The Walkerton water tragedy.* Toronto: McClelland & Stewart Ltd.

Pioneers to the present: Biddulph Township 1850–2000. 1998. Lucan: published by the Corporation of the Township of Biddulph, Lucan.

Internet References

Avro Arrow. www.avroarrow.org

Dyslexia Facts. www.dyslexia-inst.org.uk

About the Author

Photo: Roger Bullock

Terry (Terrence Patrick) Culbert was born May 13th, 1942, in London, Ontario. He is a fifth-generation Irish-Canadian. The Culbert family immigrated to Biddulph Township from Tipperary, Ireland, in 1840. At the age of eighteen, Terry left the village of Lucan to begin a forty-two-year career in television news.

Today, the father of two wonderful married daughters, Sarah Renda and Dana Johnson, Terry lives on Amherst Island at the mouth of the St. Lawrence River with his fabulous life partner Barbara Hoegenauer. The couple resides on O'Drains Bay overlooking Prince Edward County with their two Bouvier canines, Merlot and Justin, and Babe, their feline.

Terry has been a lifelong supporter and promoter of the village of Lucan. He is donating a portion of the proceeds of each book sold to the Lucan Area Heritage Donnelly Museum.